SARAH PRESTON spent her childhood at the mercy of abusers, but through love has put her life back together. She now has a successful career and a wonderful family.

Sarah's Story

They cruelly stole my childhood.
This is my story of recovery
and triumph

Sarah Preston

metro

Published by Metro Publishing
an imprint of John Blake Publishing Ltd
3 Bramber Court, 2 Bramber Road,
London W14 9PB, England

www.johnblakepublishing.co.uk

www.facebook.com/JohnBlakepub facebook
twitter.com/johnblakepub twitter

First published in paperback in 2008
This edition published in 2013

Papers used by John Blake Publishing are natural, recyclable products
made from wood grown in sustainable forests. The manufacturing processes
conform to the environmental regulations of the country of origin.

Every attempt has been made to contact the relevant copyright-holders,
but some were unobtainable. We would be grateful if the
appropriate people could contact us.

Contents

Dedication

THIS BOOK IS dedicated to all the women who, like me, have held secrets and not told anyone about them. I hope that the words I have written are helpful. Please don't cry for me. Put the past behind you, as I have now been able to do. Take a walk on the beach and bury your bad memories in the sand: with the turning tides of this world, the turmoil of the memories you have kept hidden will be swept away.

Take a deep breath, turn and walk away from them forever.

I know it is probably the hardest thing you will ever do, but you can do it. You don't have to feel like you are climbing Mount Everest any more just trying to get through each day. Trust in yourself, trust in your heart, let yourself be enveloped in the rays of a new day's sunshine. Let the healing process begin.

We – you and I – will have won our innermost battle.

No one can harm us now.

We are the survivors.

Please speak out for your rights; don't do what I did and stay silent. We have to stop this happening and protect all the remaining innocent children from the monsters that come out of the shadows to play games we know we don't want to play any more.

The thief comes only to steal and kill and destroy. I have come that they may have life and that they have it more abundantly.

JOHN 10:10

Prologue

I REMEMBER THE day like it was yesterday, as clear to me as the hours, the minutes, the seconds I have only just lived; and yet it seems so long ago – another lifetime, lived by someone that wasn't me, in another world far away from the one I know. How I wish that day had never existed; how I wish I had never known it.

It was a warm summer's day in June 1972. The sun shone bright on my face, accompanied by a breeze that made me feel refreshed and reborn. I felt as vibrant and alive as the sun, and inside my heart was sprinkled with the glow of beautiful rainbows and the softness of butterflies so delicate yet so perfect. I was eleven years old and, like so many other days, I was off school to be with my mum. I should have gone to classes that afternoon but, when Mum asked if I wanted to go to bingo with her, I said yes.

If I knew then what the next four years had in store for me, I think I would have probably begged a boarding school to take me in. Or ended my life there and then. It might sound extreme, but not nearly as extreme as the unimaginable events that were about to happen. But I didn't know that yet.

I should have put the sun to bed, dampened the rainbows to extinguish their beauty and set the butterflies free. After all, once the thief of childhood had chosen to visit me, what would I have left in my life to live for?

One

AS MUM WALKED quickly along I half walked, half ran, trying to keep up with her as her steps seemed to quicken with every stride.

I had always enjoyed spending extra time with Mum, even though I knew it was wrong and I really should have been at school. My schooling was important to me, but I still had four years to go and this seemed like plenty of time to concentrate on my education. 'Don't worry, love,' Mum used to say, 'you can catch up tomorrow.' But, as time went on, I began to realise that I would need a lot of tomorrows to catch up on everything I had missed.

I ran carefree and happy alongside Mum on that warm June day. The sun beamed down and shone bright on both of us. I loved to see the shadows I made as I ran along the pathway in front of her. On nice days like this, Mum and I would always walk down the hill, a journey that took us about half an hour. Sometimes she would tell me not to dawdle – I was always dawdling – because she panicked about missing the bingo tickets she wanted when we got to the bingo hall. I didn't know what all the fuss was about – I thought all tickets were the same apart from coming in different colours, but Mum thought differently. 'Winning tickets,' she often said, 'are better if they aren't the first or last out of the packet.' That was her explanation, and we had to arrive at the right time.

Mum went to bingo three, sometimes four times a week; she had a bingo addiction, although she would never have admitted it. It was like a drug to her: she believed she had to go because if she missed going she would miss her chance of winning. That was why she often kept me away from school to go to bingo with her. Sometimes I hated it, other times I didn't mind, but going back to school got harder each time I was away. I would find it difficult to settle back into the routine or catch up on the work I had missed. My form teacher would ask me for a note to explain why I had missed more school, but Mum never wrote one for me. 'You don't need a note. Just tell them you weren't well, it'll be all right.' But she didn't understand how strict my teachers were, or how severely I was reprimanded each time I turned up empty-handed; she didn't understand that I would never be believed even on the occasions when I was genuinely ill; she didn't understand that I could never do the homework I was set because I hadn't been in the right lessons; and she didn't understand how more and more my absences led to my peer group picking on me and calling me names. In the end, it was easier just to stay away.

And so the bingo hall – an enormous building on the outskirts of town that had started life as a cinema – became my second school. The large main hall housed the central seating area, on either side of which was an aisle and then more seats. The chairs were covered in a thick, musty, red moquette, and their arms and back were made of dark, polished wood. I suppose they were the original cinema seats – they were certainly in the traditional style, with the seats tipping up when you stood. Mum always chose the same area to sit: at the back of one of the side rows, close to the exit, and a few seats in. It was her place, and everybody knew it. And I became such a familiar face that soon nobody gave me a second look as I sat next to her, playing on 'my' tickets – used bingo cards that I had picked up off the floor where previous players had discarded them, so that I could follow the game in my own little way.

The hall was always filled with the same people, women like my mum, housewives from the same social background, filling the time before their children came home from school and their husbands returned from work. They didn't work themselves. They had no time to – they had families to look after and bingo to play. The hall was a popular destination where people went most days, nights and weekends. It was nothing special; it wasn't glamorous or exciting. It was just there, beating life into a tired working-class community, used each day and loved by those who called it their own.

One day, as Mum and I were sitting comfortably waiting for the game to begin, Jean, the lady who worked at the snack bar, walked up to our row. 'Excuse me,' she said, gesturing at Mum to let her past.

Mum smiled at her as we stood up, but once we had sat down again she started muttering under her breath. 'Why couldn't she have gone in there?' she whispered, pointing at the completely empty row in front of her. I shook my head in disapproval, but secretly I couldn't understand why she was making

4

such a fuss. Jean had bought a ticket too – she had a right to sit wherever she wanted. 'I know what she's up to,' Mum continued. 'She's just trying to be nosy.' My mum was superstitious about her bingo, and very secretive about the numbers on her tickets – she was lucky, and won more often than most, and people were curious to know how she did it. Or maybe she just didn't want Jean to know that she had a little scheme going on with one of the callers.

His name was Bill. I remember seeing him for the first time walking through the hall, striding forward with his head held high. He seemed to belong in the bingo hall, and walked with an air of importance, with the air of a man who wanted to be regarded as an important cog in the workings of the bingo machine. He was a slight man, with grey, Brylcreemed hair, glasses and silly ties that clipped on to his shirt. He was always very nice to Mum, stopping to chat whenever he saw her, but I didn't like him. I don't know why I didn't – there was something about him that made me feel uneasy. The scheme Bill had going with Mum could easily have lost him his job, so they had to keep it very quiet. He used to pay half the cost of her bingo tickets, and in return she would split her winnings with him whenever she had any luck. This became quite profitable for him.

Mum's friendship with Bill did not go unnoticed. Every time she won – which at one stage was a couple of times a week – everyone would turn round to see who had called 'house' at the back of the hall. When they realised it was Mum, they would seem annoyed – especially if it was Bill calling the game. Bill was married – perhaps that was what caused the outrage, though I suspect it was more likely jealousy of Mum's success – and he had a child. But he lived about twenty miles away from the bingo hall and, because he worked split shifts, he kept a flat locally. He occasionally went home in the week and on Saturday nights, but most of his time he spent at work. He had not been married long, and I remember overhearing a conversation he had with another employee at the hall.

'Don't you mind being away from Julia?'

'She prefers me to stay in town when I'm working,' he replied. 'Doesn't mind me being away – better for her than me going home in the early hours. I don't want to disturb her or the baby by going when they're asleep.'

I had seen his wife once when she visited him at the hall. She walked through the building with her nose turned up as if she was too good to be in this place surrounded by such people. Nobody liked her much – they all thought she was a snob. But her absence meant there was never anybody around to check up on Bill. He was free to do what he wanted, whatever that might be …

Sure enough, Bill was there that summer's day. He was chatting casually with my mum when suddenly he asked her if I might help him make the sandwiches that were sold at the snack bar. 'She'd love to,' Mum told him, either not seeing the warning looks I sent in her direction, or ignoring them. I felt so ill at ease – I don't know why – that I complained. 'I just want to stay here with you, Mum, and play on my tickets.' But she was already focused on her game, and my protests fell on deaf ears.

He asked again a few days later. Again I protested. 'Don't be silly,' Mum told me. 'I'll still be here when you've finished.'

These 'helping' sessions went on for about two weeks. Each time after helping Bill, I would go back to where Mum was sitting. He would always come with me and arrange for me to help him on other days too. Often Mum was busy – she'd be halfway through a game – so she would just nod her agreement.

I hated every nod she made, yet I wasn't sure why.

Two

I WAS BORN in 1962 in a large industrial town in the northwest of England. The town I grew up in was once alive with the sound of clogs on cobblestones and shuttles speeding through cotton looms in the numerous factories and mills that surrounded the place I called home. The cotton mills that had made this town what it was had dominated its existence for nearly 200 years, and in that time the town had grown in size so rapidly that housing was built quickly in uniform rows to house thousands of mill workers in the 1840s and 1850s.

I spent the first five years of my life in one of these houses. My memories of it are vague, but I recall the dining room well – it was used as a playroom for my sisters and me because it had no fireplace. I don't remember sitting in the lounge very much at all, even on Sundays when we were together as a family. If Dad was watching a film or a football match, we had to go into the playroom so that we didn't disturb him: he liked peace, and became very angry when he couldn't have quiet. Sunday was Dad's day.

My sister Carolyn was older than me; Gemma and my brother Robert were younger. I would have had an older brother, but he died when he was four months old. We saw our maternal grandparents regularly. I loved my granddad – he always smiled a lot and made us laugh with his funny stories – but I remember my nan being a little harsh, always finding fault with the way my mum did things. I remember them coming over one Sunday for their dinner and her laughing at Mum's roast chicken because its chest had fallen in during cooking. 'What have you done to it?' she asked.

'Nothing, only cooked it,' Mum replied.

'Well, Evelyn,' said my nan, 'I've cooked more chickens than you'll ever cook, and not one of them has ever come out of the oven looking like that!'

Dad laughed, but I could tell Mum was hurt by her words. She wanted to be a proper mum, even if she sometimes found it difficult.

Every Christmas, my nan and granddad would deliver a real Christmas tree to our house. I would be mesmerised by the smell of the pine, and would be filled with excitement at the prospect of waking up on Christmas morning to find the tree decorated from top to toe, and a stocking. It was never a real stocking, of course, just one of Dad's old fishing socks, but it was always filled with the same things: an apple, an orange, some nuts and a shilling. It was magical. As we grew older and decimalisation was introduced, our shillings became a shiny five-pence piece. We didn't always get real presents – Mum and Dad simply couldn't afford it – but we always had a good Christmas dinner. There would be lovely roast potatoes, and turkey, if there was enough money, otherwise chicken just had to do.

In the afternoon, we would sit around playing with our toys and doing jigsaw puzzles. One Christmas, Carolyn and I were given baby dolls that cried. They were so beautiful. We were never given clothes for them – that would have simply been too expensive – so I used to wrap my doll up in a terry nappy, which was just like a shawl. I used to care for that baby doll as though she was my very own child, clinging to her whenever I felt in the need of comfort, and whispering in her ear that I would always look after her. I loved her more than anything.

One day, Carolyn and I played truant. She was responsible for taking me to school, and she decided that she wasn't going to go. Impressionable to the last, I told her that, if she wasn't going, nor was I. We spent the whole day in the park, growing hungrier and hungrier, then arrived home an hour late because we had no means of telling the time. Mum was furious. As a punishment, she took away our baby dolls and gave them to a girl who lived near by. I still remember saying goodbye to mine, as tearfully as if I had been parted from a real baby.

Dad was a window cleaner by trade, and worked alongside his brother. They had a window-cleaning round on the outskirts of town and worked every weekday and the occasional Saturday morning. Every Friday night, my sister and I would stand at the corner of the square by the church railings waiting for him to come home. Mum never went out to work while we were very young. She made a bit of extra money from childminding for working mums, and I remember other children occasionally sharing our home. Then, when I was a little older, Dad stopped window cleaning because he had not been well, and we lived off state benefits. We were no different to many other families – jobs were hard to find and there was unemployment all around – and we became reliant on dole cheques and free school meals until Dad started working again at the local mill. By this time, Mum had decided to start working as well, cleaning offices in the evening, and so our care was shared between our two parents.

Our parents were strict with us. When we were naughty, we were smacked and sent to bed. We usually got smacked on the backs of our legs. Dad's hand always stung for ages, but Mum's was much less painful until she started using a slipper. Occasionally, we were belted, but we were never treated as harshly as some children were by their parents, because we were never left cut or bruised by our punishments. Still, we hated it, and I hated being sent to my room, especially during the summer months when I could hear other children playing out in the streets. I remember once going back downstairs. 'Please,' I said to Mum and Dad, 'I'll be good from now on.'

Mum was furious. She chased me back upstairs and took the handle off the bedroom door so that I couldn't get out. After she had done this a few more times, I sneaked one of Dad's screwdrivers into my bedroom. I never dared use it to escape, but it was a comfort to know that I could get out if I wanted to.

One summer, it seemed as if we were always in trouble, but I was an impressionable child – more of a follower than a leader – so I suppose it was inevitable. If someone told me to do something, I just did it. No questions, no qualms. I thought that was how you made friends. One day, I was playing with Denise, a girl who lived near by. We were hanging around on the corner of the street, just sitting on a wall and then jumping off. As we sat looking down into one of the gardens, we saw a big bush with beautiful red berries. Denise dared me to eat some to see what they tasted like. I didn't want her to think I was soft, so I put a handful in my mouth. 'Yummy,' I said to her. 'They're good.'

Denise tasted some for herself. 'They are, aren't they?' she replied.

We sat munching away on the berries for the best part of an hour before we grew bored. 'What do you want to do now?' I asked her.

'Let's go and play in the lift in the big block of flats over the road.'

'You know I can't. I'm not allowed to cross the big road on my own. My mum will go mad, and so will my dad.'

'Oh, I see,' replied Denise dismissively. 'So you're scared, are you?'

14

'No,' I told her, desperate not to seem so.

'Well then, let's go.'

Moments later, we were in the lift travelling towards the top floor. We went up and down eight times, getting out every time someone else wanted to use it. We played around for the next half an hour, up and down, up and down. Gradually, every time I went up I began to feel dizzy, and every time I went down I felt sick. We stumbled from the lift and the block of flats into the road outside, and Denise propped me up as we staggered back home. Mum wasn't at all happy when she answered the door, but one look told her something was wrong. She phoned an ambulance and the next thing I knew I was being whisked away to hospital.

The berries, it turned out, were Laburnum – highly poisonous. I was lucky to get to the hospital when I did. But it didn't stop me from being as impressionable as ever.

As bingo became Mum's life, she had to have regular trips to feed her obsession. I continued to accompany her to the bingo hall on the days she went, and I continued to be coerced into helping Bill make the sandwiches. More and more I found myself being asked questions that made me uncomfortable. 'You're very pretty,' he would say to me. 'Have you ever had a boyfriend? I bet you have.'

'Don't be silly,' I remember replying. 'I'm too young for boyfriends.' I tried desperately to steer clear of his questions, but he was persistent and continued to ask them. He seemed always to be fishing and prying for answers to questions that he had no right to ask.

'How old are you?'

'I'm eleven,' I said proudly.

'You look very grown up for eleven. I'd have thought that you were at least fourteen,' he replied with a glazed look in his eye.

It was a look I would grow to hate, the look I now know and have grown to understand. It was the look of a fifty-eight-year-old man who was planning and plotting to abuse a child.

Three

WHY ME?

I have asked this searching question so many times in my life, but I have never found the answer.

Was it something I did?

Was it something I said?

Was I smiling too much?

Was I flirting?

What was it about me that attracted people like Bill?

If I could wish and have my wishes come true, I would find the answers to these questions. And then I would feel that I had regained some of my stolen emotions and pieced together the fragments missing from my heart.

One day, Bill approached my mum. 'Would it be OK if Sarah helped me with the sandwiches a bit later? I can drop her home in the car if you like.'

Mum thought about it for a moment. 'I suppose so,' she replied. 'Just make sure she's not late for her tea.'

The afternoon bingo session finished all too quickly. Suddenly, Mum was saying goodbye, leaving me alone with this man I hardly knew but certainly didn't like. 'Come on,' Bill said and smiled his greasy smile at me, 'we need to go to the supermarket to buy the fillings.' He led me out to the car and we drove to the shops in uncomfortable silence.

Once we had bought what we needed and returned to the car, Bill told me he had forgotten something he needed for that night, and he needed to pop home before we returned. Inside my body I felt my heart racing, as though I was suddenly running a marathon. I was so uncomfortable, but I didn't know why. Throughout the journey, I felt so lost, alone and confused. Questions catapulted around in my head, making me feel dizzy.

Why was I alone with this man?

Why had Mum allowed this?

How well did she know him?

How long had she known him?

Was it long enough to trust him?

What would Dad say when I didn't return home with her?

Didn't she realise how afraid I'd be alone with this man who was, to me, still very much a stranger?

As we drew up outside his flat, he told me that the lady who lived in the house at the side of the flat was quite nosey. 'If she comes out,' he said, 'like she often does, I'll tell her you're my niece.'

I didn't understand. Why did he have to lie? Why did I have to pretend to be his niece? I certainly didn't want to call him Uncle Bill. I had enough uncles. Uncles I knew. Uncles I liked. Uncles I'd known all my life.

Just as he said she would, the neighbour came out within seconds of our arrival and stood expectantly at the side of his car ready to talk to him. He chatted to her while opening up the front door to the flat. 'Go upstairs,' he told me. 'I'll be up in a minute.'

As I walked up the stairs, I saw something that I remember striking me as being very strange. On the top step there was a big jar of sweets – the kind of jar I was used to seeing when I went to the sweet shop. They appeared to be sitting there waiting for me, as if someone had known I'd be coming along soon.

The 'flat' was more of a bed-sit, with a chair, a television and a bed all in the same room. After a while, he came upstairs and through the door into the flat. He disappeared into the bathroom, then returned a few minutes later, got himself a drink and came over to sit where I was sitting. He put his hand on my knee, resting it there for a minute or two before standing up and going to get the sweetie jar. 'Here,' he said, 'you can have some if you like.'

'No, thanks,' I replied.

Ignoring my answer, he put his hand into the jar and took out four sweets, which he placed in my hand. I didn't want them. I didn't even like that kind. 'Come on,' he said after an uncomfortable silence. 'It's time to go. We'd better hurry or you'll be late home.'

As I walked down the stairs, I felt his eyes watching me, burning into me. The intensity of his gaze made the eleven steps feel like eleven hundred. I wished, with all my being, that I was home.

I never saw that flat again. He moved shortly afterwards to a place where he said people weren't as nosey.

I started high school for the first time that year. I was very proud dressed in my new uniform, and I felt so grown up. I was moving forward, leaving the junior school behind. I'd get to play hockey instead of rounders and have showers after games, just like all the older girls. It was going to be so good, and I could hardly wait.

Mum continued to play bingo all through the summer, which meant that I was forced to carry on helping Bill make sandwiches. More often than not, he would ask Mum if I could stay on a bit, then drive me home when we had finished. I didn't like it, but Mum gave me no choice. She knew, if I helped with the sandwich preparations, he would continue halving the cost of her tickets. This was so important to Mum, especially as we got further into the week and money became scarce. One day, as we were finishing up and the sandwiches were all made, I said, 'I have to go home.'

'I need to go to my flat to get something,' he said without looking at me.

'Can't you take me home first?' I asked.

'No,' he replied, in a tone of voice that I could not refuse. 'I need to go home first, it's urgent.'

It made no sense. I lived four, maybe five minutes away by car; he lived twenty-five minutes away.

We arrived at the new flat and he parked outside. It was a large old house that had been divided up into six bed-sits. 'It won't take long,' he told me as the engine came to a halt. 'I only need to pick up my chequebook.'

'I'll wait here,' I said.

'No,' he replied quickly. 'It would be better if you came inside with me.'

I really didn't want to go inside this big, strange, unwelcoming building; I just wanted to go home. As we went up to the first floor, I felt very uncomfortable, especially when he turned the key in the lock of his flat.

'Come in,' he said. 'I won't be long.'

Inside, the flat was strange. It was a large room that had been divided up by a partition wall that had two recesses in it, making two smaller rooms. One was a small kitchen, the other a bedroom. The lounge had beige and cream flowery wallpaper, a small suite, a coffee table, an electric fire and a TV. It smelled funny. I didn't know what the smell was, but I didn't like it.

Bill walked around the flat moving pots from the night before and hurriedly shifting magazines that had ladies on the front covers without their blouses. I remember thinking, He must like to read a *lot*, given how many magazines there were. Everywhere I looked there were piles of them, all around the edges of the room. They all had ladies without their blouses on the front.

Eventually, he took a chequebook out of the drawer and put it on the table. He sat down beside me and started stroking my knee with his hand. I didn't like it and I asked him to stop, but he took no notice. I felt scared and alone. He took me over to where the bed was and asked me to sit next to him. I remember counting the ten paces in my head, trying to focus on how to get out of the room and away from him before I became too frightened to move. 'I think it's time we went,' I said quietly. 'Mum will wonder where I am.' But still he took no notice.

He continued to touch me. His fingers had long nails that scratched at my skin. Suddenly, he moved his hand up to the top of my leg and into my pants, pushing my skirt up towards my waist as his hand moved further up my thigh. 'You're very grown up for a girl of eleven,' he said, as he felt the small, newly developing hair.

Inside, I cried out loud. I felt as if I was being swept up by a tornado, trapped and unable to reach for safety.

Why wouldn't he do what I asked?

Why wouldn't he listen?

Why wouldn't he stop?

Why did he continue to touch me when I had said no?

Was a child's 'no' no good?

Inside my head, I shouted, 'I don't want this or what you're doing. I don't want a man to put his hands on me. I want to go home.' But the words remained firmly in my head: I was too scared to make a sound.

Eventually, I pulled away and started to object, clutching at my clothes and trying to straighten out all the new creases he had made in my skirt.

'OK,' he said. 'I'll take you home. Just give me a minute.'

On the way back home, I determined to tell my mum what had happened immediately. Suddenly, he broke the silence. 'Don't say anything about this to your mum. She won't believe you.'

The words came out of his mouth, echoing into existence as I sat stunned and shocked by what he had done to me. I could not believe what I heard. Did he honestly think such a warning would make a difference to me? Surely Mum would believe me. Wouldn't she? Now he had sown the seeds of doubt in my mind, what could I say, how could I tell her?

He repeated his warning. 'No one will believe you.'

Every word he had spoken I heard over and over again, sounding out like a loud bass drum in my head. Louder and louder the words became, until they reached a pitch I couldn't stand any longer.

I arrived home at a quarter past six, just as it was getting dark. I looked at Mum, and she looked back at me. I felt that she could see the desperation building deep in my eyes, but she never asked me if I was OK. She just looked away and carried on with whatever she had been doing before I came in.

Did she know then what had happened?

Did she have some idea before I could tell her?

Bill had followed me into the house. As I looked at Mum, he looked at me. 'Same time tomorrow, Evelyn?'

'Yes, that's fine,' Mum replied. 'See you at bingo.' And he left.

I felt lonely standing there in the kitchen, as if someone had placed me in a home that wasn't my own. I went to my room and my sister was there. 'Hiya,' she said brightly. 'Want to play?'

I wanted to tell someone. In that one moment, for a split second, I didn't care about what he had said, I just wanted to tell someone. Gemma was the only one around, but she was younger than me. She wouldn't understand.

And then my moment of confidence deserted me. Perhaps what Bill had said was right. Perhaps no one *would* believe me.

I cried into my pillow that night. Dad came in when he heard me. 'Are you OK, Sarah?'

'Just a bad dream,' I lied, hoping Dad wouldn't want to stay with me.

'OK,' he answered, and closed the door quietly behind him.

That night, I learned how to cry myself quietly to sleep. It was something I would get very used to over the weeks, the months and the tragic, lonely years that followed.

Four

AS AUTUMN TURNED to winter and the days grew darker and colder, Mum still played bingo as fanatically as ever. She was always desperate for a win. Sometimes when she asked me to go, I lied and said I had a tummy ache. She would get annoyed with me. 'You were OK this morning, why are you suddenly ill now?' But there were days when I had no choice, especially if Dad was working the afternoon shift at the mill. I had to go with Mum because she couldn't leave me at home alone.

Bill continued to halve the ticket costs with Mum, and in return I got to go to the flat with him twice a week, lost, lonely and very confused. Every time he took me there, I wanted to run away from him, but I didn't know for sure where I was or how to get home. I remember feeling that I had to get away and escape, but each time we drove home he went a different way to confuse me, so I could not remember the key places we passed. It was hopeless.

As the hours of Bill's abuse mounted up in my young life, what he did to me become more distressing. To start with, he just used to touch me using his fingers, but soon enough something seemed to change. He became more purposeful, as if he did not want to spend the same amount of time taking me to the next level as he spent getting this far. One afternoon, back at his flat, he told me he wanted to show me what a penis felt like. 'I want you to know how it will feel inside you,' he told me. At first I didn't know what he meant, but I soon realised when he removed his trousers.

He took off his underpants and stood before me, a weedy little old man with the funniest legs I had ever seen – I remember them to this day, although at the time, of course, I saw nothing funny about them – and a penis that resembled a shrivelled-up old prune.

'You're going to be a grown-up now,' he told me in a quiet voice I will never forget as long as I live. 'You'll be a lady.'

He moved closer and closer towards me that rainy

afternoon, saying he wanted to 'enter me'. I remember crying, begging him to stop, but he paid no attention. 'I knew we'd be perfect,' he told me. 'I knew we'd fit together perfectly.'

I was silent that afternoon as he drove me home. He tried talking to me; in fact, he continued talking all the way home. I stayed silent. I had nothing to say. I knew now that he had wanted to 'enter' me for weeks. He had just taken his time, and now my time had run out. I felt soiled, cheap, dirty and alone.

As he pulled up outside the house I got out of the car. 'Bye, Sarah,' he called breezily. 'Thanks for your help.'

I went inside the house without even looking at him. I was glad nobody was around to stop me or speak to me. I went into the bathroom and scrubbed myself raw, making sure I cleaned everywhere he had touched me. I could even feel his touch under my fingernails. I used the hardest nailbrush I could find, the one Dad used after potting his plants, and the coal tar soap that I hated the smell of. Anything was better than his smell. It was a ritual I would continue each and every time I went home from Bill's house.

As I look back on the events that changed my life forever, I feel as if I cheated on myself. Why? Because

I never cried out or shouted out for help. It's a small word, just four tiny letters. 'Help.' One day when I was alone, I wrote the word in big capital letters.

HELP.

But, when I read it out, it didn't sound any louder.

In my heart I yelled, and my voice echoed as though it came from the Grand Canyon itself, echoing to everyone I knew. Every day he came for me, I yelled louder and louder inside. And yet, after Bill's warning to me, I never dared say that little word. And, if you don't say it, no one will hear. His warning that nobody would believe me was attached to me, weighing me down like a huge boulder chained securely around my neck.

Why was I never rescued?

Why did no one hear me?

Why did no one come?

Why did no one stop him hurting me?

Why did no one care?

I saw Bill the very next day. He looked at me, smiled and winked. He held my secret, but he never let it show, continuing as if nothing had ever changed. I knew my life had altered forever; he just carried on regardless. He continued his conversations with my mum about how lucky she was at bingo; he continued halving her ticket costs; and he continued, with her unwitting support, taking me back to his home. There was never an occasion when he took me back to his flat that abuse did not occur. It was the only thing he seemed interested in, with the exception of the Saturday-afternoon football. It became a weekend ritual: he would wash me, abuse me, then sit down in front of the television to watch the match. I would have to sit there with him, watching, waiting, reliant on him to take me home. If it hadn't been for Saturday football, I would have been home that bit earlier, washing Bill's smell off me once again …

As the days and weeks passed me by, I felt that I was no longer living my own life but taking part in someone else's, the life of a complete stranger, a person I knew nothing about. Everything I knew about being a child, a young girl embarking on the journey into her teenage years, became a blur, disappearing from my memory like fragile snowdrops melting. My life before Bill became a smoggy memory drifting out to sea.

I wondered what I had done to deserve this treatment. Why did another person, especially a grown-up, want to do such unspeakable things to a small girl? I asked these questions inside my head, listening intently for an answer, but no answers came.

Shortly before my twelfth birthday, I started my periods. I knew a little about what was happening, but no one had ever told me the facts of life, I never really knew what to expect. I didn't know what was happening inside my developing body, I just learned as I lived.

Bill appeared as normal at the house that Saturday morning. It was earlier than usual. He often came early at weekends to pick me up to help him 'make the sandwiches' – Saturdays were always a hectic day both at the bingo hall and for him generally. After all, there was football to be watched. Bill had to make sure everything was prepped early because he always needed extra sandwiches at weekends. He also did his shopping on that day for him and his wife. I still got to 'help', but it was usually after I had been to the flat and he had done whatever he needed to do.

I hated Saturdays. They lasted longer.

I didn't tell Bill at first about starting my period. I waited until we were at the flat. He came up to me and led me to the bed, a bed that I found more repulsive each time I saw it. He tried touching me, but I pulled away, rejecting his advances, and he became angry. 'I've got my period,' I told him defiantly. 'You can't touch me.'

The change in him was terrifying. His face became distorted by rage, and he seemed a different man to the one I vaguely knew. He had become even more of a monster, desperate for revenge. He stood up, moved a couple of steps away from the bed, then turned and looked at me for what seemed like hours, but I suppose it could only have been a few short moments; then he stamped away from where he had put me and moved into the lounge area. I slowly rose to a sitting position on his polluted bed, and as I did so I began pulling at my skirt to hide my exposed body as best I could without making any sudden movements.

Bill turned around, gritting his teeth so hard I thought he'd lose them. He was so irate, his whole body seemed to shake with rage. I thought for a moment that he was going to hit me. Instead, he stared at me, clenching his fists against his sides. 'Why didn't you say before I drove you here?' he asked. His resentment was clear in each of the words as he spoke them.

Suddenly, I was delighted for the first time in months. So delighted my heart lifted a little while it was moving out of the storm clouds. He couldn't touch me. I was momentarily free from him. Free from his touch. Free from his smell. Free from his poking and prodding and his evil ways. I had won, for a little while.

My heart didn't stay lifted for long. I soon realised that he was counting the days of my menstrual cycle, like a man possessed, waiting patiently for the all-clear. At the end of the week, he had called in at Mum and Dad's with a look of glee in his eye, and before the hour was up I was once again back in the flat, desperate to break away from him. I was a prisoner once more, a caged bird unable to use its wings to fly away from the impending dangers. I was trapped in a spider's web, held fast in the delicate weave, danger vibrating through each silken thread that I felt underneath me.

As he did what he did, touching me and moving on top of me, he began talking to me. 'Do you know that it's safe now?' he asked me.

I didn't want to talk to him while he was touching me, so I never answered him, or even asked what he meant.

He spoke again, smiles curling at the corners of his mouth as he did so. 'I could come inside you … and you wouldn't get pregnant because you've just finished your period.'

I struggled beneath him, but he held me fast. All I

could think about was that in twenty-eight days I would be free again. Free to live and be a child, a normal child, even if it was for only five short days.

I remember clearly wishing a wish that day. I know it was stupid and, dear God, when I think of it now I know the thought would be unimaginable for any girl. But my wish that day was that a period could last forever.

Five

AS THE WEEKS and months continued to pass me by, I felt I was no longer living a life but an existence. I was there talking, moving, eating, sleeping and breathing the same air as everyone else, but I felt like I was no more than a visitor to a world I hardly remembered.

Mum and Dad started arguing more and more, and to my young eyes it seemed that their marriage was breaking down. Dad was made redundant from his job at the mill, and Mum blamed him because once more they didn't have enough money coming in. Day in, day out, the same arguments would be repeated. Our house sang out each week with their constant accusations. I hated it. I felt as if I had become embedded in a war zone.

One day, Bill came round to ask if Mum would be at bingo later on. He wasn't interested in her, of course; he just wanted to know if I would be along for his sick, perverted ride. Dad was still in a foul mood from one of their arguments that morning. He nearly exploded when Bill opened his mouth. I knew it was best to stay out of the way in these circumstances because in the past my sisters and I had all been pasted for getting in the way when he was angry at Mum. And Dad hit hard: his handprints usually lasted on our legs for the whole day.

Dad was so angry he screamed at Bill to get out. 'She won't be going to bloody bingo ever again,' he yelled.

Normally, I would cringe in fear whenever Dad shouted like that, but suddenly I felt jubilant. If Mum couldn't go to bingo, I wouldn't have to go to Bill's. Perhaps the abuse would stop. He had become more intense over the last few weeks. He had even forced me to watch him ejaculating. I had always looked away. I couldn't stand seeing him, holding it, pulling at it while he grunted like a pig.

My euphoria only lasted a few short minutes. Mum followed Bill out to the car, as I watched from the bedroom window that overlooked the front garden and our street. She stood there talking with him for what seemed like forever. I was desperate for him to drive away, but he kept glancing up at the window when he realised I was watching them both. Suddenly, I saw him pass Mum a five-pound note; she slipped it into her overall pocket, all the while looking round to see if Dad was at the door.

My feeling of jubilation sank to the soles of my feet and slipped quickly through the carpet and down between the cracks of the floorboards. The wonderful feeling I had felt for a few short minutes was lost to me forever.

That very afternoon, when Dad was out in the back garden in his greenhouse, Mum went out to see him. It had been two hours since they last spoke, and I knew she hoped he would have calmed down. He talked sharply to her, but I could tell by the tone of his voice that his temper had subsided a little. Mum told him that she was taking me to the shops down the lane and that we'd walk there and back so we would be out a couple of hours. He seemed to accept that we'd be doing what Mum said; he even gave me ten pence for some of my favourite sweets. In fact, I think even I believed I was off to get some shopping. After all, it was clear we couldn't afford bingo, and Dad had been very clear that she couldn't go – perhaps Mum had just borrowed the money off Bill for groceries. Maybe my father, in his anger, had unwittingly put an end to my ordeal. Perhaps I was being protected before anyone even knew I needed protecting.

Sure enough, when we left the house, Mum took me straight to the sweet shop. She sent me inside to get what I wanted while she waited outside. As I walked into the shop, I knew instantly what I would buy: sherbet. I loved sherbet, little fine crystals of sugar candy in all sorts of different colours. I particularly liked the rainbow candy best. It didn't taste any different to the plain pink sherbet, but it looked prettier in the big jar high on the shelf. As the lady in the shop poured my sherbet into the weighing pan, I watched in childish wonder as the different colours of the rainbow mixed and blended together.

After I had been served, I went back outside to where Mum was waiting, my bag of sherbet grasped tightly in my hand. She held my hand and started walking in the wrong direction for the shops, but I didn't realise where we were heading until I saw the bingo hall in the distance.

I felt numb inside. Mum had lied to Dad; but she had lied to me too. I was being taken to the bingo again. I hadn't escaped at all. As I looked up, I felt a little better when I couldn't see Bill's car in its usual spot; but I hardly had time to breathe a sigh of relief before I saw it appear from a side street and pull into the car park.

I started kicking my heels and dragging behind Mum. 'Don't dawdle!' she shouted at me impatiently, and pulled at my arm.

As the years have passed by, I sometimes wonder whether Mum would have acted differently if she had known what her 'friend' was doing to her daughter. Perhaps I have no right to suggest that she wouldn't have protected her child; but I know that, at times, especially when things were not going well with Dad, bingo was the only thing that really mattered to her.

Once inside the bingo hall, Mum queued for her tickets. I could not believe I was there, a prisoner once more. I saw Bill walking to the stage where the calling machine was. This was a big machine that had all the different-coloured numbered balls in it. It was standard practice to turn it on five minutes or so before the game started, and I remember wishing I was the heaviest ball trapped in the machine. At least that way Bill wouldn't be able to get his hands on me. I heard the sound of the air blowing in the machine, but I didn't look up. I watched Mum instead because I knew that if I looked at him he would smile at me.

I hated his smile more than Bill himself now. I saw things in his smile that other people didn't see. To me, it wasn't a friendly smile but a smile that said, 'I'm going to abuse you again today. I'm lucky. I've got a girl no one else knows about. I can do things to her and no one can stop me.' It was a smile that reflected his perverted, immoral pleasure. Every second of his smile seemed to me to last an hour.

That afternoon, after the first half of the bingo had been played, he went to talk to Mum while I was getting a drink of orange from the snack bar. As I opened the door leading back into the hall, he was standing in my way on Mum's aisle so that I couldn't get to my seat. 'Excuse me, please,' I said, as politely as I could.

'Hello,' he replied brightly as he moved slowly to one side. I still couldn't get past him, so he moved again. This time I could get past, but as I did so he moved at the same time as I moved into my seat, and I felt him push slightly against me. I wanted to cry out loud, but the warning bell inside sounded louder than ever, echoing inside my head over and over again.

'No one will believe you.'

Sadly I knew Bill was right. No one *would* believe me.

It was too late.

I didn't see Bill for three days, which was unusual because he would often come to the house every other day. When he finally appeared, Mum called me in out of the garden. I saw him standing there smiling at me and my legs turned to jelly. 'Bill wants you to help him with the sandwiches today, love,' Mum said cheerily.

'Do I have to? I don't feel very well.'

'You'll be OK. You'll only be out for an hour.'

I started to feel angry. I hated her. I hated them both. Why wouldn't they listen to me? But yet again I said nothing. Yet again I had to go with him. I had no choice.

I knew the sandwiches weren't on Bill's agenda the moment we drove past the bingo hall and the shop he usually bought the fillings from. 'Why did you lie to my mum?' I asked him. 'Why aren't we going to make sandwiches like you said you had to?'

Bill didn't reply. He just continued to concentrate on his driving and smiled at me again when we slowed at the traffic lights. I couldn't stand it. I wanted to jump out of the car but, as I put my hand on the door handle, he leaned over and locked the door.

'I don't want you falling out, do I?' he chuckled.

When we arrived at his flat, I noticed something different. Everything was in its normal place, but there was a towel placed on the bed. He made himself a drink while I stood by the chair, my nervous fingers fiddling with the cover on the back of it. I wanted to leave, and I told him so, but as always I was ignored. He didn't want to waste time talking – he had other more important things planned for me that day.

He took hold of my hand and led me over towards the bed.

I pulled my hand out of his.

I didn't want this to happen again.

He took me firmly in his hands, laid me on the bed and slipped my pants down. 'I'll just be a minute,' he said matter-of-factly. He turned away and I struggled to find my pants and put them back on when he came back with a bowl of water and some soap.

I was confused. What was he planning? Why did he want the water? I soon found out. He started to wash me down below. 'I've had a bath,' I told him angrily, pushing his soapy hand away from my body. He ignored me and continued applying the soap and working it around my intimate parts. He seemed to be enjoying this, but I didn't understand why. Grown-ups do weird things, I remember thinking. Gradually, he started putting his fingers inside me. I thought of other things – nothing in particular, just anything to make my mind leave the room.

After about ten minutes, he rinsed and dried me. Then he kneeled in front of me on the floor and took off his trousers. He started taking out his penis, and asked me to hold it. Play with it.

Why would I want to? I had dolls to play with. I didn't want to play with this.

I felt revolted and sickened by his request, but I knew he would get angry if I didn't do what he asked. It felt weird. I had never felt anything like it. I pulled my hand away, but he grabbed it and put it back on him, this time holding it in place with his hand over the top of mine. 'Do it like this,' he said, as he guided my hand up and down. He started to breathe heavily, and funny stuff appeared. He told me this clear liquid was just as dangerous as the other stuff that appeared later because it could make a baby. I pulled my hand away.

'I don't want to make any babies.'

He laughed.

I detested him.

He was vile, stupid and an idiot.

I wanted to hit him.

I wanted to hurt him like he was hurting me.

He took me home about two hours later. I had noticed that he seemed to be keeping me at the flat for longer and longer. As usual, the first thing I did when I got in was to have a bath. I scrubbed my hands with Vim, desperate to wash off all of him by scrubbing off the layer of skin that had been in contact with him. Dad shouted at me for using all the hot water. Mum wasn't best pleased either as she had washing to do. I was sent to bed for being inconsiderate and for not asking before I used the water.

I hated them all.

I went upstairs, closed the door, got undressed and jumped into bed. I picked up my newest Enid Blyton book, *The Naughtiest Girl Again*.

I stopped reading and began to think. Had I been a naughty girl for using all the water?

Why was it always me that seemed to be in the wrong?

Was it all my fault?

Six

A FEW MONTHS later, Mum did what I was longing to do: leave home. She had come to the end of her tether with Dad and all the anger and arguments. She packed her bags and upped and left. I wanted to go too, but she wouldn't take me; she just took Gemma with her, and promised to come back for me the following week. But she didn't keep her promise, and she never came to get me. I only saw her about once a week when she came to visit.

She moved into a flat close to town with a friend of hers, and not long after that she met another man and moved in with him. But she never once came back for me. She never rescued me. She left me behind, and the washing, prodding and poking of her twelve-year-old daughter continued.

I had been Bill's victim for over a year now. Every night I made myself ill trying to think of ways to escape him. I even tried telling him I was still on my period one week, but I knew it was only a matter of time before he became angry with me if I did that, and with the anger came a look in his eye that was so frightening that I went with him the next time he asked.

I knew that the time would come when he would hurt me, and I was proved right soon enough. He had washed me as usual – this was something he did now every time he took me to his flat. I was convinced he thought I was dirty. He then lay beside me and pushed himself into me, entering me with such force I cried out in pain. I begged him to stop but he just continued heaving himself up and down on top of me. As he became more aroused, he pushed deeper inside me, hurting me so much I felt as if he was tearing me to pieces, ripping out my life. He moved out of me quickly and immediately ejaculated on my tummy. It was a sickening feeling, and my stomach churned harshly. I wanted to wipe it off with my hand but I knew I'd be sick if I touched it.

I wanted him off me. I pushed him away but he

pulled me back towards him. My dress had got his 'stuff' smeared all over it, and I wanted to tear it off quickly. The cloth felt wet against my legs. He tried to enter me again, but I pulled away. He grabbed me again, held me tight and kissed my mouth. He tasted sour and vile as I felt his dentures against my lips. He then asked me to touch it, his penis, but I didn't want to, so he pushed my hand on to it, holding it with his hand over mine. I refused to move my hand, so he moved it for me. 'It's better if you hold it close to the top,' he said breathlessly.

'Please,' I asked him – no, begged him – 'let me get dressed.' I desperately wanted to put my pants back on.

He shook his head. 'What's started needs to be finished,' he told me.

I tried to pull away once more, but he was too strong and my body hurt.

He started to make himself hard again by touching himself, pulling and tugging at his penis, and then he moved higher up on top of me. He kneeled up on the bed and put himself close to my mouth.

I was so scared.

I closed my eyes.

My body cried.

I wanted to swallow but I felt too sick.

I couldn't swallow, something horrible was in my mouth, making me heave. It seemed to last forever. I managed to push him away. 'Leave me alone,' I yelled in my head, but no words came out. 'I want to go home.' I didn't hear these words either.

That evening, I was late home. Dad wasn't happy – he had made my tea and now it was ruined. 'If you can't get her home at the right time,' he told Bill angrily, 'she's not going again.'

I didn't see Bill for almost a week, but I was too scared to be glad. I knew from past experience that he would soon be back.

I hardly saw my mum over the next couple of months. She was too busy enjoying her new life with her boyfriend. I remember thinking at the time that she didn't really miss me, and had never really loved me. If she had done, she would never have left me. She would still be here caring for me. Maybe, if she hadn't deserted our family, I would have gained the strength and courage I needed from being with her to stand up and speak out about what was happening to me. Instead, I was shown how weak she was. She didn't want to stay with Dad and work things out; she just decided to leave when things got wobbly at home.

Instead of being loved, I remained frightened,

rejected and unwanted. I was only a little girl. Why did my mum choose to walk out on me when I needed her the most?

Inside my heart, I felt so very, very alone.

Spring passed in what seemed like a few hours. I enjoyed spring, but there were of course parts of it that dragged like a never-ending cold winter's day: those times I spent with Bill.

Finally, summer arrived. I liked summer too – I enjoyed helping Dad in the garden on long, hot days. It was my responsibility to help the tomato plants in the greenhouse to cross-pollinate. I used to do this by tickling the flowers on each of the plants with a feather Dad had given me. I used to laugh when I thought about tickling the tomatoes – it always seemed a daft thing to do. I would fall asleep quickly at night – as I closed my eyes, I would hope for a sunny day tomorrow. At least then, when I got home from school, I could help Dad in the garden.

Why do dreams shatter like glass before you get a chance to live them?

For a few days, I had been aware of feeling somewhat uncomfortable around Dad. I would occasionally catch him watching me, looking at me for longer than he normally would, with a strange look in his eye. I began to sense something was wrong, and my young mind started working overtime. Was he tired of having me around? Was he going to leave me too, just like Mum?

I was woken early one morning by Dad standing at the side of my bed. He was wearing nothing but his underpants. 'Sshh,' he whispered as he gathered me up into his arms. 'Don't make a sound, or you'll wake Robert.' My little brother was still asleep.

What was wrong? I wondered. Had something happened? Was Mum back?

Dad walked the short distance across the landing and carried me into his and Mum's room. I looked at the bed expectantly, but soon realised that Mum wasn't there after all. It had been an idle hope.

Dad laid me on the bed, then climbed in beside me and kissed me on the cheek. I was still very sleepy, but I managed to say to him, 'What are you doing, Dad?'

He shushed me again.

I very quickly realised what he was going to do as he wriggled in the bed beside me, taking down his pants.

Oh, God. No! Not you too …

I wept silent tears all the time my dad was touching me. I whimpered and gasped out when he pushed inside me, but by this time I was awake enough to notice the look on his face. It was a look of surprise: I hadn't cried out, and he could tell that I wasn't a virgin. He carried on regardless, unconcerned about who had taken his daughter's innocence before him.

Bill's warning screamed inside my head. Would his warning become Dad's warning too?

I wanted to be free.

I wanted to escape.

I wanted to end my life.

I wanted to die.

I wanted to be an angel. No harm would come to an angel.

My whole world had been falling apart for over a year, but now it was collapsing quicker than ever before. I heard voices in my head asking the same question over and over again.

Why me?

Why choose me?

The words echoed inside my head, moving around like a carousel until finally I fell back asleep, sobbing and crying silently in my own bed after my father had carried me back there half an hour later.

Seven

I WOKE THE next morning in a world that had become even more of an unbearable dream, a world that my own father had invaded in a way that should never have happened. I knew that a father should be someone you look up to, someone who takes care of you, protects you and comforts you when you fall down or hurt yourself.

A father should never look on his daughter as an object he desires, like he might a passing woman. Not even for a few short, stolen moments.

He should not see his daughter as a substitute for the lover he can't secure when his wife has left him.

A father needs to be just that: a father, a friend to his children when they are at their lowest. Times like now. My father should have remained my friend. Instead, he crossed a boundary that had already been transgressed, a boundary that should have remained intact.

My dad's abuse only happened twice more.

Only twice …

I didn't know what to do to make him stop. I couldn't stop Bill. And now I couldn't stop him.

On the next two occasions when my father carried me gently, cradled in his arms like precious cargo, into his bed in the early hours of the morning before my brother woke in the next room, I still wept silently. But no one heard, and Dad didn't stop. He didn't even stop when he saw my tears falling on his pillow. My father only thought of himself. His needs, and his desire to do evil things to me rather than playing nicely with his daughter and taking care of me the way he should.

When he had sex with me, I believed that, if I moved under him the way Bill had moved on top of me, he would be satisfied and leave me alone. But he didn't. He started talking to me the same way Bill had, speaking in a low voice that sounded unfamiliar in his mouth.

It didn't sound like my dad. He had become a stranger.

'You've done this before, haven't you, Sarah?' he asked me on one occasion.

'No.'

'I know you have. I can tell.'

I hid my face by turning it into the pillow. I didn't want him to see my lies, or for him to kiss me like he had done the time before.

'I don't like it, Dad,' I slowly said to him. 'Please stop.'

But he just carried on moving up and down, grunting and groaning. He was heavy. I felt him press against my body in the same way Bill had. I wanted so desperately for it to stop. As my sobs grew louder, he angrily pulled himself off me then carried me back to my bed and left me sobbing into my pillow. He said nothing as he closed the door behind himself.

He never, ever said, 'I'm sorry, Sarah.' Not that night. Not ever.

When I was old enough to think it through, I blamed Mum for what happened with Dad, because she had been the one to leave us. I blamed her for not being a wife to him. Somehow I think I tried to avoid blaming him for anything. I don't know why. But, when I look back and try to examine my thoughts and feelings about what happened to me all those years ago, I think I did blame him once, for a short time.

I wanted to know why he had not helped me. He knew I had had sex. He knew someone had abused me, that someone had taken his little girl's virginity. He found that out when *he* abused me in the same way. Yet he did nothing. He never came to rescue me.

He couldn't save me. If he had taken me to the police or to social services, he was in danger of being found out himself. He didn't protect me because he was so busy protecting himself. And he must have known it was Bill who had abused me; there was no one else it could have been. But he stood by and did nothing.

The daughter he once knew had gone forever, and he had helped with the abduction of her childhood.

The weeks passed. Mum still only came to see us once a week, but Dad was talking to her more now. One day, he even asked her to come home, but she said no. He wasn't happy, and that night he was still angry. I could see in his eyes that he was thinking through the events of the last few months, replaying the arguments they had had over and over again in his mind, wondering what he had done that had been so bad that she had decided to leave him and – what was worse – move in with another man, sharing a bed that was not his.

He wanted Mum to come home. He missed her. It was as if she had rejected him completely this time, and the challenge of another man who was living with his wife and receiving all her attention only made my father angrier.

I wanted her to come home too, but for different reasons now: then, at least, Dad would stop taking me to his bed. After all, she was his wife, not me. Wasn't it time she took back her role so that I could try and become a child again?

At least if Mum came home I'd be safe from one lot of abuse.

Wouldn't I?

As I lay in bed at night, I tried to make sense of everything that had happened between Mum and Dad. I listened intently when I heard Dad's footsteps on the stairs, urgently hoping they wouldn't stop at my door. I would breathe a sigh of relief when I heard his door close and again, a moment later, when his light switch flicked into the off position.

I lay back down and continued to think about the mess I was caught up in.

Why would she not come home?

Who had done the most wrong in their marriage?

Was it her for playing bingo too much and spending all their money?

Or was it Dad and his temper?

Why had he become so irate over the last few months?

Why was my mother not spending time in my father's bed?

These questions climbed aboard the carousel that was already travelling through my mind fully laden with my other questions.

I tossed and turned for hours until early the following morning when I finally slipped into an erratic, hazy sleep.

One morning, Bill turned up earlier than ever to ask Dad if I could go and help him make sandwiches. I was furious when I saw him. What was he expecting? Extra time after his usual games? I didn't want to go. I wanted to stay home – although why I wanted to stay home was beyond me.

If I went with Bill, I'd get abused. If I stayed at home, I'd probably endure the same fate.

Was there no way out? Was there no escape route out of this mess of a life? As I lay on my bed listening to their voices below me, I found my mind slowly drifting, asking yet more questions about myself.

What was it about me that these older men found so interesting? Why did they want to do these horrible, unjust things to me? Surely it would have been more fun for them both if they had gone out and found a *real* woman each. Perhaps they were both afraid of women their own age. Or was it simpler than that? They both knew that women who were not attracted to them could easily reject them; but with children it was different. A child would never go against anything an adult did.

I woke suddenly from my daydream to hear Dad's voice in the kitchen. 'Yes, course she can, Bill. She'll be happy to help.'

What was this? Paedophiles United? Had they both formed a club that I was a member of, but not considered worthy enough to have a vote? They never even asked me if I was willing to play. Dad had volunteered my 'help' to Bill. Yippee, I thought, time to get clean again. I can hardly contain myself.

I wondered then if he would have volunteered me knowing what Bill had planned for me. I was still deep in thought a few minutes later in Bill's car. Were they both unsure of me? Was Dad worried I would tell Bill what he had already done to me? Was Bill worried I may have told Dad about him? They both had reason to panic. After all, I was a bomb of information, information that could see them both sent to prison. Both of them held my secret, and I held both of theirs. But I couldn't tell anyone about it – now more than ever, because if I did I would be left with a broken, torn world in which I would have to survive alone, unwanted and unloved.

I had to come to terms with not being wanted. Mum had come back and taken Robert with her, but still I was left behind. Alone with Dad.

Why didn't she want me?

Was I not good enough?

Perhaps she knew what had happened to me?

Was I too dirty now?

Was I so bad that she hated me?

Mum said she thought I'd prefer to stay with Dad, and that he should at least still have one of us there with him.

She said she knew I was safe there.

How wrong can a mother be?

Some days my dad was wonderful, kind and considerate. A reminder of happier, more innocent times. Times that were lost forever, never to return. But other times I caught him watching me, and I knew it was only a matter of time before he would come back to my bedside again, haunting my waking moments more than ever.

Dad and Bill had become quite an enterprising team while Mum had been away. Dad was growing lots of flowers and Bill was selling all the surplus ones for him at the bingo hall. Bill had always admired Dad's chrysanthemums and dahlias in the garden and offered to sell some to friends and people he knew at the bingo. Dad was over the moon when Bill called back later that day with news for him: he wanted a further ten bunches of flowers in addition to the fifteen he had already taken and sold.

As Dad was in such a good mood, Bill asked if I could help him do sandwiches for the snack bar again. Casually, Dad replied, 'Yes.'

Had Bill planed this? Was he really selling Dad's flowers for him? Or was he paying to have his special treats with me? I felt like I was being bought and sold, not unlike the poor flowers that had been cut away from their secure stems, only to wither and die in a vase on a windowsill, away from the fresh air and the garden they knew as home.

I ran into the bathroom and tried to vomit, but nothing happened. I was anxious for the sickness to start — at least that way I knew I would be safe. I put my finger down my throat but I couldn't do it: I was too much of a coward to go the whole way.

Dad had let me down yet again. He knew what Bill intended to do to me.

Hadn't he learned my awful secret the hard way? Hadn't he found out the truth through his own abuse? Why hadn't he stopped me going? Did he want Bill to touch me? Did he find pleasure in knowing Bill would be touching me?

That afternoon, alone with Bill in his flat, I felt more secluded than I had ever been. This time he sat me on a chair by the fire. He got some of his magazines off the top of the tallest pile – this pile was half my height, such a lot of magazines – and opened one of them. He started to look at it while he rested his hand on my leg. He wanted me to look too, but I turned my head away.

I didn't like the pictures inside. All the ladies were either bare or just wearing some lacy knickers. I remember thinking they were very pretty, but why did they have their hands on their boobs? Why are they touching their bodies in those places? Bill smiled at me as he looked through the pages. He moved his hand up my leg and pulled off my pants. I wanted him to stop, but I knew there was no point asking any more. 'Be quiet,' he said, when I asked him to stop.

He always did that.

He always told me to be quiet, as if I had no

rights, not even the right of speaking or hearing my own voice. He had a way of looking at me that made me very anxious; his eyes were warningly dark and unsettling. His gaze carried harm that told me he could hurt me more than he had already, if that was possible.

He continued to look at the magazines the whole time I was there that day, and I knew I had to look too. Each time I tried averting my eyes, he just moved the magazine further across my lap so I couldn't avoid it. I tried to move further away from the magazine but his hand held one of my legs and the chair arm crushed the other, making it impossible.

He wanted me to talk to him, tell him what I thought about the images in the magazine. I stayed quiet when he asked me questions. I didn't want to talk about these things. Bill always talked and he always made me feel intimidated and afraid when he spoke the way he did. I began to drift into another world, my secret, safe world that I didn't let anyone else into. Is that what I'll look like when I'm older? I found myself wondering when I saw a picture of a lady with her legs slightly open. I didn't want to look like that. I didn't want any of it. It was yuck.

Bill put the magazine down and picked up another one. He led me to his bed. I had to put his thing in my mouth like in the picture. I closed my eyes. I didn't want to see it. I felt as if I was choking and my body began to shake. He pulled it out of my mouth and put his hand on to it, pulling the funny outer skin back and forth. Over and over again, he moved his hand, back and forth, back and forth. He groaned as he ejaculated all over me.

I slid gently away in the hope that he wouldn't feel the movement while he had his eyes closed. This way I didn't get too much stuff on me. I hated him doing this. I wanted to fall through a hole in the floor and be swallowed up so that I didn't exist and wouldn't have been subjected to this vile, contemptible act of indecency.

He took me home an hour later and picked up the flowers from Dad. Then he left.

Eight

I HAD HAD a particularly disturbing week.

For any other child my age it should have been an ordinary time, when they would have been happy being a child, in their homes surrounded by their loving families. Spending time with their dads. I dreaded being alone with mine.

What had happened to my loving family? Why, in such a short time, had my world been changed beyond recognition? Were my sisters, my brother and I to blame for our parents' separation? Or was it just my fault? Was I being punished because I had done terrible things?

I did still love my dad, but I hated the night-times.

I found myself fearing the long, lonely hours alone in the house with Dad more than the abuse I constantly received from Bill. I just wanted a 'normal' dad, not this dad. This dad was a stranger. He had appeared in my life and replaced the father I knew so well when I was ten. The father that had cared for me so well in all the years before this one arrived had disappeared out of sight.

Thankfully, he started staying in his own room at night and didn't venture into mine. I was so grateful. Was my old dad finally returning? I smiled a little smile when this thought pushed its way past all the others to get to the front of my mind. Had he realised what he had done was so wrong?

Bill, however, was a different story. He would visit me three times in five days and, as much as I wanted to plead with Dad that I shouldn't go with him, I found that, in my desperation, the excuses I came up with were not logical or believable enough. I remember saying that I had to water the plants in the garden and those in the greenhouse too. It had been such a hot day, and Dad had said they were my responsibility. I was stupid really – I should have realised that Dad wouldn't have minded watering the plants in my absence.

I told him I couldn't go because my friend Paula

was coming round to see me. 'She'll call back,' Dad would say.

I hesitated, taking my time looking for my sandals. I could feel Dad's eyes watching my every slow, calculated move. I began to look for my sandals in all the places I knew they weren't. 'Just get a move on, Sarah. Bill hasn't got all day.' His voice carried a threatening edge with every word he spoke.

I remember thinking I was glad Bill didn't have longer to spare than the stolen two-hour slots he so very kindly devoted to me. I just wished he would give them to a charity shop instead.

The first time I went with Bill that week, he had wanted to ejaculate over me not once but twice. He made the same request on the other two visits. Each time I objected, saying I wasn't feeling well, but he just went ahead and did it anyway.

The next morning, as I opened my eyes, Dad was there, pulling back the bedclothes and scooping me up. I started sobbing loudly. 'No, Dad. Please, Dad …' Although I was complaining louder than ever before, he continued to carry me into his room. I kicked him as he put me down on the bed. I knew I had hurt him, but he told me to be quiet. I tried to jump out of the bed but I couldn't get past him – he was too strong and he pulled me back down. He held me down with the weight of his body and I was just too small and too weak to fight back. There was no way I could lift a grown man off me.

There was no hope. I knew I had to stay put and tolerate his pleasure and my pain. I was conscious that I had to do something, anything to stop this happening again. I couldn't be a victim any longer. I was not going to give in. *Not this time, not again.*

I cried hard and I cried loud – as loud as I thought was safe. Safe enough that the neighbours didn't hear, yet loud enough that Dad would think they might.

He was so shocked by the noise I made. I cried out again, but this time I used words, not just sobs and tears. 'Get off me, Dad! Leave me alone!'

It worked. He moved, but as he did so he spat out the most hateful accusations to me, in a voice that made me shudder with fear. 'I suppose you don't say no to him, do you, Sarah?' he hissed.

'It's not my fault! I want it to stop!' I cried out with a gentleness that made my voice so low it was barely audible, but I know he heard my words. 'I want it *all* to stop,' I pleaded through the stinging tears that were now wetting the pillow. I hoped that he would realise I wasn't just talking about what he was doing but Bill too; if he did understand, he never confirmed it. He just looked away from his twelve-year-old daughter lying on his bed with her nightdress up around her waist.

Dad never returned to my bedside any night after that. At last I had freed myself from one of my abusive tormentors. I was safe in my home once again and I hoped I always would be.

At the end of the week, Mum came to see Dad. They talked for a long time alone in the lounge with the door shut. A couple of hours later, Mum called me into the lounge and told me she would be coming back home the next day.

I was so glad. At last I wouldn't be alone any more.

I was growing up. My body was developing and inside I had emotions that I could not understand. No one talked to me, or explained the changes that were taking place. I had picked up key words by listening to girls talking in the showers after games at school. But I knew that, without the knowledge and understanding of what they meant, these words would be no use to me. I didn't know what to expect as my body grew and changed, but I felt that I knew more than most of my friends about the development of a man. Things I knew I shouldn't have known until I became a great deal older.

I only knew that sometimes I felt funny inside when

I was touched in different ways. Bill made me feel funny and I despised it, but I couldn't understand why I felt like that when his fingers touched certain places.

I didn't like it.

It wasn't right.

Why give me these feelings when I don't want them?

I wished I could lock them up in a box and take them out when I felt it would be safe to handle them, although I imagined I'd probably never be able to. I asked so many questions then, not just questions about my body – which I usually asked a friend about – but also questions about the exploitation I endured. But the latter questions were always silent ones, spoken inside my mind and never, ever aloud.

By the time I was thirteen, I had done everything I could think of to try and escape from the world that Bill and my dad had created for me, but the more I tried, the more trapped I became. If I said I was unwell and couldn't go with Bill, he just came an extra night the week after, as he would after I'd had my period. It was his way. He was sly and sneaky and well practised in the art of paedophilia. There was never any escape. Every corner I turned, I knew all too well that he would be there, watching, waiting, ready for his reward.

This man I loathed so much had become more

devious and cunning than he ever was before. He seemed to want more and more each time he got me alone in his flat, while I found his need to be with me unbearable, nauseating and beyond belief. He constantly wanted to spend time alone with me, so much so that his desires to see me more began to make me feel weighted down. His needs were making my whole, poor weary body plummet to the bottom of the deepest ocean. Bill really was becoming overly obsessed with me. He had a power over me that had the unique strength of storm-driven waves crashing against unprotected, eroding chalk cliffs. I felt like I was tied to a jealous boyfriend whose obsession was spiralling way, way out of control.

I wanted so much to be free, yet every thought I had about becoming so was blown away like small, inconspicuous specks of chalk on each fresh, newly initiated breeze, heading towards the mightiest of hurricanes in some faraway place.

I was so tired of trying to break free from both of them. I had had the hope drained from me, and I began to feel as if Bill and my father had captured everything from me that there was to capture, and more besides. I felt like they had bottled my willpower and sold the last bit of soul I had to the highest bidder.

One day, when I was feeling especially low, my friend Lucy asked if I would like to go to a disco near to where we lived. It was on Saturday night at a local church hall, St George's, and everyone, she said, would be there. By everyone, she meant all the nice, good-looking boys. Guys she knew I would fancy if I ever saw them. The problem was, Dad didn't like me going out, especially to places he knew I would meet boys.

Lucy was a lovely girl. She was slightly taller than me with blonde shoulder-length hair that hung straight around her slim face, and blue eyes. She was so pretty. She had a radiant smile that was filled with warmth and caring, and just being in her company made you feel alive. She loved the disco, and she loved the attention boys gave her as her figure began developing curves in all the right places. Lucy spoke with such enthusiasm about the disco, and I knew this was just the distraction I needed, a distraction I hoped would take me back into the world I had long since left behind.

Up until that point, I had had no experience of boys my own age. I was still very much a little girl, content to read Enid Blyton books in my every spare moment. I didn't think about boys much. I just wanted to be a part of the world I knew my favourite characters were in. I would have given anything to go out on a sailing boat on my very own Sea of Adventure. At least if this dream came true I would be out of the clutches and touches of my tormentor forever.

There were boys I came into contact with each day at school, but I was always very quiet and shy in front of them. Because of this, the boys always called me names. I can't remember ever doing anything that would encourage their name-calling, it was something they just did. Every year at school, someone always became the bullies' victim. I don't know why they chose me. I had a little bit of acne — a few spots on my chin and two on my forehead. I think at the most I had six pimples — nowhere near as many as some of the other, popular girls — but it was me they called names and me they all picked on. These boys never seemed to pick on the popular girls who I often thought were quite mouthy, uncouth and not really very nice at all. They were everything I wasn't.

I always felt alone at school, but Lucy helped. She always listened to me and usually advised me with her pearls of wisdom whenever I spoke to her about a problem I had. 'Not to worry,' she'd often say, 'they'll stop picking on you eventually. You just have to ignore them.' So I never retaliated. But, when they were supposed to get fed up and stop, they never did. Ignoring them just seemed to fuel their need for more.

I was their new pawn in a game they insisted I took part in.

I couldn't escape.

That Saturday night, as we left home giggling and excited, deep inside I felt a bit apprehensive and anxious about going out to St George's, but Lucy made me feel better by telling me that the majority of the boys who went there were from the Catholic school, not ours. I remember my heart feeling lighter that night, for the first time since all this began. Up until then, I hadn't really noticed boys before. I was just a girl who liked to read and I enjoyed being alone. After school, I played in the street with other kids who lived near us, but after dark I was usually indoors. I didn't socialise or go anywhere with other girls or boys my age.

Dad had insisted I be back home by nine; Lucy was allowed to stay out until ten. I decided to go, even though I knew it would take forty minutes to walk home. For the first time in over two years, I felt free that night. I knew Bill couldn't interrupt this moment. He wouldn't be coming to get me, not tonight – no one could take this time away from me.

The church hall was very busy that night. There were lots of teenagers there, people I didn't know, and I felt shy. The boys looked at me, moving their eyes up and down, and I felt embarrassed. The heat around me seemed to raise my temperature. I began convincing myself that they knew all about me, even though that was impossible. No one else knew because *I* hadn't told them yet. I felt like I was at an auction waiting to be sold to the highest bidder.

Lucy knew lots of people because she had been there before. She introduced me to some of her friends, girls as well as boys. We got into a little group and, after chatting, we all danced for quite a long time. It was late when I looked at my watch and my heart hit the floor: it was half past eight! I would never get home in time. I said goodbye to Lucy and the others and ran the three miles home. Dad wasn't happy when I arrived home five minutes late and he sent me to bed. I was grounded for two weeks. Two miserable weeks.

I lay in bed cursing the unfairness of it all when it suddenly hit me. I would be free of Bill for two weeks. My heart jumped for joy and silently I whispered, 'Thanks, Dad' to myself.

I would be free of Bill for two weeks.

I went to sleep that night smiling.

I was silly, really. I actually thought that the grounding would include the daytimes too.

Nine

BILL ROLLED UP outside the house at 11.30 the next morning. Dad had told me to weed the front garden but I wasn't allowed in the street to play. As Bill got out of the car, he said he was just going to say hi to Mum and Dad, then we'd be on our way. As I heard his words, my heart was leaping, yet when I answered him the rest of my body was shaking and trembling in terror. I knew he would not like what I said to him.

'I can't go with you,' I said. 'Dad grounded me last night.'

He was so angry and it showed – if he could have spat feathers, he would have done so by the pillow load. He marched hurriedly to the front door, knocked and walked in. 'Hi,' I heard him call, trying to hide the undertones of anger from creeping into his usually cheery greeting to my parents.

'Hi, Bill,' I heard Mum reply. 'Do you want a cuppa?'

He accepted. He knew how to play this game – he had done it before.

'Are you going to bingo, Evelyn?'

'I'm not sure, Bill.' That usually meant she wanted to go but she wasn't sure if Dad would give her the extra money.

'Will it be OK for Sarah to come too?' He paused slightly, before quickly adding, 'I could do with a hand with the snack bar again.'

I quickly ran into the room from behind the hallway door where I had been listening in on their conversation. 'I can't go, can I, Dad? You've grounded me.'

'That's a shame,' Bill replied.

'Oh, let her go,' Mum said to Dad.

'But, Mum, I'm grounded for being in late. I can't go out,' I told her.

Dad looked at me, then at Mum. 'OK,' he said, finally.

What had he done?

Why was he doing this?

Why was he punishing me in this way?

I went with Bill again that day. He was all over me now. He was more intense. He poked and prodded me like stock at a cattle market. Every touch, every move, every kiss from his moving dentures and every immoral whisper he spoke into my ear made me feel sick deep inside. He made me feel as dirty as a mechanic's oily rag so overused it was unpleasant to hold.

Once upon a time I was better than this. Why had my life changed so much?

This wasn't the life I belonged to.

This wasn't where I should be.

I didn't want to be a toy for a perverted old man. I wanted to have a normal friendship with a boy my own age. I wanted to discover sex and all that goes with it with him, later.

When I was older,

When I was ready,

When *I* said it was time.

I didn't want him to continue stealing my virginity. I wanted it back for the man I would grow to love, marry and be with forever. I wanted so desperately to become the child I never was, the child I never had a chance to become. I had lost the true me; no one would ever know that person or hear about her achievements. That Sarah had been cut down and left to die. She had been discarded like a fallen branch on a forest floor, already thick with hundreds of other fallen branches, useless to the tree that had lost it.

I wanted to be set free. I wanted to fly away gently like a butterfly into a world where abuse never happened, where children could be free to be children.

Where children were children.

Is it so wrong to wish for these things? To want a life that belongs to you and only you. I had dealt with all of this by myself for such a long time. No one knew what had happened to me, apart from my dad, and he was too busy protecting himself instead of me.

It was now almost winter and I was looking forward to Christmas. Dinah, a neighbour who lived across the road from us, had two young children under five. She and her husband Simon enjoyed going out at night and often had a babysitter in to watch the children when they weren't there. One night, they were let down and their babysitter couldn't make it. Dinah came across and asked Mum if I could sit for her. I had never babysat for anyone before, but Mum said I would be OK – I was sensible and I could always nip back across the road to get her if there was a problem.

At seven o'clock, I went across the road to Dinah's house. The children were both in bed and asleep, so she left to meet her friends and Simon met up with the guy from next door who he regularly went out to the pub with. I sat and watched TV for the rest of the night. Mum popped in twice to see if I was OK and at half past eleven Dinah arrived home, thanked me for sitting for her and paid me two pounds.

I was delighted. At last I had money of my own. When I got home, I hid it safely in my bedroom.

I remember my thoughts that night; they remain in my memory as clear and as sharp as all the others. If I got to babysit again, and if they paid me, I could save the money and this could be my escape fund. I could go anywhere, do anything. I could get away from them all. I had already made plans to run away when I was old enough so that I could escape them all. The only problem was that I would have to wait three long years before I became sixteen.

I babysat a few more times for Dinah and Simon and was paid each time. On one occasion, Simon came across quite late in the evening asking if I would sit for them. Dinah had arranged to go out and Simon should have been staying in watching the children, but his friends had called round for a beer and were going into town. Simon wanted to go with them too. He looked at me hoping I'd say yes. 'OK,' I told him, 'I'll be there in a few minutes.'

Simon was delighted – he was able to go out with his mates. I gathered my homework and went across to their house. After he left, I locked the door and checked on the children – they were fast asleep. I got a drink from the kitchen and settled down to do my homework. It was so quiet and peaceful. It was nice to be somewhere I felt safe away from Bill.

A few hours later, Simon returned. He was quite drunk and was laughing. After a few minutes, he got some change from his pocket and paid me my babysitting money – 'a little extra tonight', because it was short notice. Three pounds instead of only two. (I know Dinah would have only paid fifty pence more.) He followed me to the front door but it was still locked, so he fumbled in his pocket to get the key. He leaned over me to get to the keyhole, then lost his balance and stumbled. He fell against me. Suddenly, he pushed his stubbly mouth brusquely against mine as he straightened up; I tried pushing him away but he was heavy. 'Simon, you're drunk,' I said to him.

'No, I'm not. Come on, you know you want to …'

His voice slurred from the drink. 'You're a big girl now, come on.'

I cried as he tried putting his hand up my dress and into my pants. I dropped my schoolbooks. As I leaned forward to pick them up, I smelled his breath, which was so repugnant I began to feel nauseous. As I straightened up, he still had his hands on me, pulling all the time at my clothing.

I tried pushing him off me again. He was too hefty, too strong. He pulled at my pants and they came down at one side. I begged him to stop, but he didn't. He continued with his task regardless of the fact that I was a child almost young enough to be his daughter. He started to fumble with the zip on his trousers.

The drink inside him made him sway. I begged again, pushing him away as best I could, and he sloped to one side. I knew this was the opportunity I was waiting for, so I seized the moment. *This was not going to happen to me again.* I was going to be in control this time. As he straightened up, I lifted my knee up hard. He fell over in pain.

I pulled open the door and ran home. I never slowed down for any of the sixty steps it took to reach my back door.

Simon may not have been as old as Bill or my dad, but he was still twenty-seven, fourteen years older than me. What gave him the right to try it on and attempt to have his way with me, the same as the others?

I was a child.

A child.

Not a grown woman.

Sex wasn't on my school timetable.

Was I not entitled to decide what I wanted to happen to me?

Did my opinion not count?

This time I won. I had stopped the inevitable from happening. I was not going to be a victim again. But that night I still found myself thinking about the same questions I had asked myself many times before.

Why me?

What was it about me?

Why choose me?

What had I done to deserve this?

Why did all these older men like me so much?

How much more could these men steal from me?

Did I have anything left to give?

Would they leave me with anything left to give?

I cried that night, like so many nights before. In between my tears I hoped that sometime soon my life would once more be a beautiful thing that was worth living – each new moment spent in sunshine and warmth instead of darkness and shadow.

Was this too much to ask?

Would my wish ever be granted?

Or was this simply too much of a miracle to expect?

Ten

AS I APPROACHED my fourteenth birthday, I realised that my life was a complete shambles. I didn't know who to turn to for help or which direction I should aim for if I wanted to run away. I was completely alone in a world populated by men who had destroyed any happy childhood memory. I was drawn into and caught up in a web thickly woven by perversion and mockery. All I wanted was to be left alone. But that would never happen.

Bill had me in his grasp, a grasp that was as difficult to escape from as an airtight room with a nest of scorpions standing guard at the door. I forced myself to think of ways to break free from him, but so far anything I thought of just sounded so far-fetched I knew the ideas wouldn't work.

One day, on my way back from school, I met a boy called Tom who lived on the estate. He was a good-looking boy, with blond hair and blue eyes, and he was quite tall for his age. He was almost two years older than me, in his final year at school. I knew the moment I saw him that he was the boy I would fall in love with.

Tom became my first true love. He helped me forget my other life. When I was with him, I enjoyed living. He made me feel like I was special, like a butterfly opening its wings for the very first time, ready to reveal its true, unblemished, perfect beauty to the waiting world in its shadow. He knew nothing about my past, and I didn't want him to know all the sordid details. I didn't want him to be ashamed of me or hate me for the things I had 'allowed' Bill to do to me. I thought, if he knew about all that, I would lose him, and I couldn't let that happen – not when I'd only just found him.

As our friendship grew into a boyfriend–girlfriend relationship, Tom and I began spending more and more time together. During the week, he would come round to my house when I came home from school and we would sit and watch television together. Sometimes I went to his house too, although his brothers would tease us constantly all the time we were together.

As winter turned into spring, we went out and walked a lot. We enjoyed going for walks, and I was always especially keen when Tom suggested them because I loved to escape from my world that held sordid secrets and the shadows of shame. We often walked down to the river with Tom's friend John, and sometimes we went as far as the paper mill. It was a long walk to the mill – it usually took about an hour and a half to get there – but it was worth it. It was so tranquil and beautiful walking along the river and back through the woods that flanked one side of the mill. Tom and I used to sit on a fallen tree and talk for ages, often forgetting the time as our long conversations rambled and ended as we came closer to share our special kisses. It was a different world by the paper mill, a world I knew to be safe, and one that I wanted to stay a part of forever. I never wanted Tom to take me home. I wanted to stay there by the river forever.

I often sit and think back to that precious time when everything was all right. I find myself remembering the look on his face when I always wanted to stay out longer. I wondered if he knew the reason I didn't want to go home. Had he ever guessed there was something so very, very wrong there? Would he have protected me if he had known my reasons?

The answer to that question I now know to be yes. I never told him what had happened; I just know he would have helped me. He was just that kind of boy. One who protects. Someone who would wrap you up in a soft blanket that was made of a material that could not be penetrated by the outside world. Tom always hated getting me home late, he always wanted to do what he knew to be the right thing; he always wanted to please my parents; and he never wanted to upset my dad. During the time we were together, he showed me kindness and consideration. He was both caring and gentle, and he provided me with the love that was so missing in my life. He was always protecting me and piecing together the broken fragments of my heart. He made me feel whole.

We spent a great deal of our time talking, but we also had kissing competitions to see who would stop kissing the other first. We usually lasted twenty minutes, although once we kissed for twenty-five. We never did anything else – it was wrong to do anything else, and we both knew that. One night, though, I unzipped my cardigan a little further than I normally would have worn it. Tom had been resting his hand on my tummy for ages, in the little space between the waistband of my trousers and the bottom of my cardigan. I thought he wanted to move his hand up a bit, but how wrong I was.

I thought I understood, but I didn't. I thought I knew what men wanted, but I didn't know what Tom wanted. I hated myself from the moment I moved my zip. I began to think he would think I was a cheap slut.

'Why did you do that?' he asked.

'What?' I replied, acting a fool, pretending not to know what he meant.

'You know, move your zip.'

I hesitated before I answered. 'I don't know, I thought you wanted me to ...'

He sighed, and I started to get quite tearful. The words that followed, the words he spoke, were so precious I couldn't speak to him for ages I just buried my head deep in his shoulder and cried uncontrollably. 'I don't want to take advantage of you, Sarah. I love you. I want to wait until we're both old enough. That's a special time and should be saved for honeymoons. Our honeymoon, a honeymoon we'll share when the time comes.' He bent down and kissed me gently.

I couldn't tell him why I was crying. As he watched my tears fall, he looked confused but I told him I was fine. Tom looked down at me snuggling into his shoulder and smiled gently at me, smiling his special smile. Whenever I saw that smile, it swallowed me whole and took me into a world away from the real one, a world of complete safety like the world we shared at the paper mill. Safe and secure, away from all the monsters and thieves I had come to know so well in such a short space of time.

A few weeks later, Tom gave me a ring that he had had made by a jeweller in town to his own design. It had five small stones set into a central square, with two collars on each side of the centre. On each of the two collars were two stones, and the smaller collar had one stone inlaid. It was so precious, as precious as the life we shared. I couldn't wear Tom's ring on my left hand, but I wore it on my right instead. It meant so much to me – for once I felt as if I wasn't worthless. I felt my life had been given back its meaning.

One evening, Tom came to the house early. He saw Bill dropping me off and wanted to know who he was. I was frightened because I knew that Tom could be hurt by what he saw, and I never wanted any hurt to touch him. I certainly didn't want the memory of Tom and Bill together in the same space by the house.

So I told him a lie.

I didn't want to, but I didn't know what else to do. My own insincerity cut through me like a hot sword through a delicate, newly carved ice sculpture. 'He's just a friend of Mum and Dad's. I sometimes go and help him from time to time.'

I knew by the look on his face he would not leave it at that. I sensed that he didn't trust Bill. He knew from what he had seen that Bill was trouble for me. Inside my body, deep within my soul, I cried out in desperation. 'Go with your instinct, he *is* a bad person.'

He looked at me at that moment, but heard nothing.

I spoke again in my mind, and then I heard myself whispering the words I wanted Tom to hear. 'Go with your instinct.' He heard nothing. I should have spoken again, but I couldn't. I didn't want to cause him pain. I didn't want to taint his world with the contaminated, spoiled stains of mine.

He asked questions about Bill later that night, when we were alone together. I felt deep inside that he did not truly believe me. I hated lying to him but I knew the truth would destroy him more than my lies, and he would leave. Tom was my only salvation in a time of crisis. I didn't want to lose him, but I felt the pain of separation even then before it happened: we were going to drift apart. I knew it was only a matter of time, and I wouldn't be able to stop it. Bill had started a heartache within us both that would lead to heartbreak for both of us.

He had won again.

A few weeks later, Tom called round to see me like he usually did on Monday nights. He started talking to me about going into the army. He said he wanted a career – a career with a future that was good for him and me. He didn't want to become trapped in a dead-end job with no prospects. He wanted to make something of himself.

I didn't want him to go. He told me he had already been to the office in town and they were interested in him. They wanted my Tom. I knew even then that I was losing him. It would only be a matter of time before he would be gone from my life forever. Lost in a new world that I had no part in.

Tom had the papers to sign within a few weeks of his interview. I cried so hard that night. They were taking away my only friend. They were stealing my first love. I was being robbed once again. Just a few weeks later he was posted to the army training camp in Aldershot. I saw him before he left to start his training. He came to the house with a large carrier bag, inside which was his Womble. It had been made by his aunt and was very dear to him. He told me that his Womble would be there for me to cuddle in his place.

I held it close. It smelled of him.

After Tom left, we wrote regularly while he was training, and I saw him twice when he came home on leave; both times he saw Bill leaving the house. I don't know what he thought, but each time he looked hurt. He seemed different after his visits – something had changed but I didn't really know what. I just didn't understand.

I lost him, as I knew I eventually would. My confidence and my new life and feeling of freedom disappeared with him. The hitherto undreamed-of chapter of happiness ended abruptly before it had a real chance to begin. I cried so much that the heartache became unbearable. I was once again free to be thrown to the lions, and no one was there to help me loosen the locks on the cage.

I was once more at the mercy of those who would steal my childhood. It was now only a case of when would the thief be calling?

I tried so hard to escape Bill and his regular visits. He even made advances while my mum and dad were in the garden. One night, soon after I saw Tom for the last time, I swallowed thirty of my dad's anti-depressant pills and some paracetamol. I waited for what seemed like forever for them to work. They didn't. Why wasn't this quick? It was in the movies. I remember feeling great disappointment that I was only a little bit light-headed. I decided that, as I still felt reasonable, now would be a good time to say my goodbyes, so I went to Lucy's house to bid her farewell.

It was two hours since I had taken the pills. As I approached her house she was just going in, and she knew something wasn't right. She watched me trip on the step and fall forward on to the sofa as I went into the lounge. 'Are you all right?' she asked me.

'I'm fine.'

'You haven't done anything stupid, have you?' my friend insisted.

As I was about to answer, my tears started to betray me. Her mum was in the other room. Lucy ran to her and she called an ambulance. Ten minutes later, I was on my way to Casualty, blue sirens whirring above my head in panicked unison.

It was a long night – the longest I had lived through

– but all I really wanted to do was die. I had my stomach pumped, and spent the next day with a psychiatrist who wanted to know why I had tried to take my own life.

I made excuses. I lied. He asked more questions, but the lying became easier with each lie I spoke. I lied my way through question after question. I had to: I heard Bill's warning over and over again in my head. I never told the truth. I kept their secrets hidden deep within me.

Bill's secret.

Dad's secret.

Simon's secret.

My secret.

I had a brief chance to expose them all while I was in a place of safety, but I didn't take it. Why? Because I was scared what people would think of me.

And because *I* let it happen.

And because *I* didn't stop them.

Eleven

MY CHANCES OF escaping had been taken from me. I wanted so badly to have been successful. I didn't want to continue taking part in a life I could not control or had no control over. Everybody else was in control of what happened to me – Mum, Dad, Bill – they all had a say, yet none of them showed any interest in my voice. My voice was never listened to, never heard. It was as if all my words were silent.

They all asked questions in turn about why I had taken the pills, but I never told them. I kept my reasons for attempting suicide to myself. It was the best way. After all, they had had chances to change my life but had not taken those chances.

Dad had a chance not to abuse me.

Bill had a chance to change his mind before starting out on the path that led him to abuse an eleven-year-old girl.

And Mum could have not given in to her bingo addiction as much as she had done.

I had no intention of talking to any of them about what I had done. I kept my thoughts to myself, safely tucked away from each one of them. I wanted to lock and block them all out of my memories before they had a chance to enter. Bill must have realised it was him that had made me feel like this, but he never said anything. He was solely responsible for me wanting to end my life, but he never seemed interested in what I wanted, just in what he could get. He had become more focused on his needs and his needs alone.

As each new day drew to a close, adding itself to the pile of all the other used and abused days in my life, I wanted so desperately to exclude him from any future memories that were being made in my life. I wanted to turn into the child I had never been. I wanted to become the rightful owner of my possessions: my life, my body and my mind. All three belonged to me, but all three had been stolen, leaving me with nothing.

No one ever even asked if I minded.

Who had given these men permission to steal away from me something that was more precious than brilliant gold or the finest cut and polished diamonds? I wanted so much to take my life in my hands and polish out the deep, disfiguring flaws that had been created within it, flaws that had with time felt like they had become lines and wrinkles embedded in my skin. I prayed a prayer for forgiveness and another for salvation. I didn't really know what or in whom I believed back then, but I had always prayed. But after a while I decided that there must have been someone in more need than me, because, even though I kneeled and prayed, no one ever replied.

No one let me know it was going to be OK.

No one heard my cries for help, carefully wrapped in each prayer.

Maybe I'd done too good a job wrapping them up ...

My dreams had not materialised; they had lain like the rest of my life in shattered pieces, like a broken mirror or a delicate piece of china. Lost forever, unable to be mended or repaired because a small chip was still missing.

I had to do something. I knew deep inside that my heart could not take much more of this torment and punishment that was given to me as regularly as my breakfast, dinner and tea.

How could I stop it?

If only I knew.

I searched for the answers again but, like me, they were lost too.

Bill was always there. He was a presence that had become my permanent shadow – a shadow that either appeared in person when I was awake or in the dreams that frequently haunted what little sleep I managed to get. It felt as if I was living a terrible nightmare that I hadn't woken up from. I had to do something fast, but I didn't know what. Experience told me I was on my own, while desperation kidded me that I had the help of an entire army to fall back on. But how could I summon an imaginary army?

I knew I should have been trying harder, but how do you rid yourself of a plague that is destroying your life with a force you have no chance of stopping because you are still nothing more than a child? How could I stop him now after three years?

I had been trying for so long to make things right. Bill was set in his own routine: he would pick me up, go straight to the flat, do whatever he wanted – which usually included the washing, oral sex and sexual intercourse – and afterwards he would kindly drive me home again, as used and abused as usual.

Making the sandwiches was now just a front, an excuse so that Mum and Dad didn't stop me going with him when he asked. Each visit to his flat got gradually worse. Most of the time he would wash me obsessively. He ejaculated on to me more times than I care to remember and he subjected me to oral sex until I hoped I would pass out. He was now sixty-one years old; I was still only fourteen.

Why did he do these things?

What did he get out of it?

Did he do this for fun?

Did he really enjoy doing this to me?

Why did he not have a normal relationship with his wife?

Why was he attracted to me?

Why did he abuse me?

Why did any man abuse a child?

Maybe he didn't see me as a child now. I was growing up, developing into a young woman. Did he now see what he was doing to me as being OK?

I tried to uncover answers to these questions but I never found a way. Many times I wanted to ask him why, but, as I approached the verge of letting the words form, I looked at him for a split second and I saw that look in his eye, the look that made me fearful of him. It was as if I would never know, never understand the truth. I asked myself then as I have asked myself now: did I really want to know why? What would I gain from knowing after such a long time?

I had to try and be stronger than I was. I had to find a way to beat what was happening to me. I asked for help each night before I closed my eyes. Again and again I asked. In the end I knew no one would answer me.

Why?

Because I had not told them. I hadn't told a single soul about this.

How could I find help if they did not know?

I began to block out my memories of abuse, clearing my head in order to become a different person. I felt stronger now, but still I remained frantically hysterical about people finding out about my life. I didn't want Bill coming to the house. I didn't want my friends to see me getting into his car. I didn't want to face questions. I didn't want to pretend we were related so that any questions they might ask would stop. I didn't want them all to know.

I didn't want to be called a slut. I had heard some girls talking about a girl in the year above me who had slept with an older boy. They had called her a slut. They said it was a name she deserved. It continued throughout the autumn term and into the next one too. Was that what I was? A slut? No, I knew deep down I wasn't; but sometimes I just felt as if I was.

I couldn't do anything about what was happening to me, even though I had gained a feeling of strength. It felt like a truckload of strength, but it wasn't the right kind. I just had to figure out how to turn it into the right kind.

I started to realise that Bill would never willingly release me from his controlling clutches. My body felt as if it was bound tightly to him by chains that only I could see. The chains felt real. The weight of them multiplied, crushing me day by day, swallowing any strength I had newly found.

As hard as I tried to make up plausible excuses not to go with him, each time he called at the house or saw me with Mum at the bingo hall I always failed in my quest to be free of him. He became the successful one every time. Mum always dismissed my complaints and said whatever I had to do would surely wait. Wasn't it more important to help a friend?

If only she knew the truth. The only way I was

helping him was by not telling anyone. By being too afraid to tell anyone, and, more importantly, growing more afraid with every passing minute.

I was keeping his secret.

Keeping him safe.

Keeping Bill from being found out.

Keeping him from being caught.

Keeping my abuser from jail.

I was protecting a paedophile.

I had been protecting a paedophile for years.

I wondered if Bill knew other girls. Other girls he was abusing. Others he wanted to abuse. In my heart and deep down within my soul, I hoped there weren't. I hoped he hadn't. I hoped he never would. But he had always spent so much time with me I don't think he would have had time for any others. If Mum had not been so insistent on me going with him all the time, I knew he would have had the opportunity to get to more girls, who would be subjected to the same nightmares I had already lived.

Did Bill's abuse of me for almost four years protect them? I just did not know.

As I grew up, I seemed to understand the wrong more clearly. The questions inside my head were not being answered but the wrongs appeared to be getting more comprehensible. I had to do something before I became trapped forever.

I came up with a plan. Lucy had visited earlier and had told me about a new church disco; it was in town, which meant catching the bus. It was held three times a week, on Wednesdays, Fridays and Saturdays. Lucy said it was great – she had been the week before and she wanted to go again this week. That night we asked my mum and dad if they would let me go too.

'How much is it?' Dad asked.

'Fifteen pence to get in on Wednesdays and Fridays, twenty pence on Saturdays,' Lucy replied. 'Plus bus fare to town,' she quickly added.

'What time will you be going and coming back?' Mum asked.

'I would have to leave at quarter to six,' I said.

Lucy looked at me, puzzled, but like a true friend she said nothing. She knew we didn't have to leave until the twenty-past-six bus, and it would not take me thirty-five minutes to get to her house.

'And we'll be back for ten if we can go,' Lucy continued.

'OK,' said Mum and Dad together, 'you can go on Wednesday as long as you're home on time.'

I was overjoyed. At last I had found a way of not being around Bill on Wednesdays. *He always came on Wednesdays.*

It was one of his days.

On Wednesday evening, I was getting ready to go out when Bill called at his usual time. Mum met him at the door – she was just about to leave the house to go to the shop. I was so glad I'd delayed her by talking to her. She explained to him how I was going out with Lucy and wouldn't be able to help him. I heard raised voices. Luckily, Dad was out the back so he couldn't hear. Bill was getting angry at Mum, telling her that he had already paid for her bingo tickets once that week, so he expected me to help him with the snack-bar preparations. Mum told him she had already promised I could go with Lucy. He muttered something and went hastily back to his car. As he looked up, he saw me watching him from behind the upstairs bedroom curtains. I jumped back in shock when his eyes looked straight through mine with an intensity that hurt. He had a look in his eyes that was worse than anything I had seen before.

It terrified me. I felt every muscle in my body tense up. It was a look of hate and anger all in one. Bill would be calculating his revenge. He would get back at me; he always did. I tried not to think about it. Yet at the side of my mind his look crept into position, waiting to be brought forward to take centre stage in the dreams I was yet to have.

Bill was still angry with me for not going with him when I went out again the following Wednesday with Lucy, avoiding his visit a second time. The following Friday he called half an hour earlier than normal. He told Mum he had extra to do and asked if it would be OK if I stayed with him for longer than usual. He also said he was going on holiday the following week for five days, and asked if it would be OK if he took me out as a treat for helping him so much. He wanted to take me to see where he was staying on holiday. I didn't want to know where he would be and wished wholeheartedly that Mum would say no to his stupid request. If I didn't know where he was, I could freely imagine he was on the other side of the world, far, far away, unable to get to me easily.

I just could not believe it when Mum readily agreed to his suggestions. Even Dad agreed too.

Had I heard right? Had they both said yes?

Bill was furious with me when he got me alone. He told me I was selfish and horrid for not going with him. After all, he had given me some spending money. In fact, he had given Mum the money, but it seemed to be the same thing to Bill. If I wanted to have some more money, he told me, I had better make sure I didn't let him down again.

Was he now in the frame of mind whereby he thought he was paying Mum for my body? I felt like a cheap, backstreet, overworked prostitute, his very own working girl. I hated what it meant. I hated even more how it felt. I hated him for turning me into someone who would be seen by people I met as having no morals.

I wanted to curl up and die.

As each day passed I made secret plans. I never wrote them down because I didn't want anyone to see them. These were my plans, plans that I knew would be destroyed instantly if anyone saw them. I kept my plans locked and stored away in a special box deep inside my head where only I could access them.

This box was kept with all the other boxes I had already stored away within my memory. Boxes were safer. No one could see them; no one could get into them except me. My boxes held furtive memories, secretive memories that, with time, had become bulky, heavy and unbearable. Secrets that weighed me down. The first box held my questions, questions that would be set free from the individual compartments they were placed in, and the box they were secured in, when at last I found the answers.

The second box was filled with all the bad, unthinkable memories of my life. In my mind I didn't keep this one locked; it was always kept with its lid slightly open so that other bad memories that were still being created could be slipped in.

In the third box were my good memories. This box was smaller than the other two. It didn't have a lid. It didn't need one. It would never be overflowing. The good memories that were there already barely covered the bottom. There was lots of room in this box; it was just good memories that were hard to find.

I knew I had to set a plan in motion. I decided to help Mum and Dad lots more than usual in the house and garden. Helping in the house was Mum and Dad's rule; it was the same for us all. We all had one room in the house to clean at weekends before we did anything we wanted to do. If I wanted to go out, I had to do extra jobs for them, as well as my usual weekly tasks. By helping them a little more, I was using up as many of my free hours as possible doing chores. If I did extra work in the house, Mum and Dad would realise I had done enough jobs to earn a little extra money to be able to go out with Lucy much more than before.

Over the next week I worked harder than ever. Every spare moment I had I did jobs around the house. I did all the ironing, the washing too. I even changed all the beds for Mum. And I worked hard in the garden once I had finished all Mum's work. Dad was away fishing with his brother for a couple of days so I mowed the grass, weeded the garden and watered all the plants in the greenhouse.

My plan worked. Although I had seen Bill four times the previous week, the following week I only saw him twice because I went to the disco with Lucy with the extra money I earned.

I was so excited that I had managed to remove the chains for a couple of nights, yet I remained slightly subdued knowing that Bill wasn't that far away and he could shatter my plans at any moment. I may have managed to escape him this week, but could I do the same next week? Would I be strong enough to succeed a second time?

As I lay in bed and the house had been quiet for what seemed like hours, I sat up in my bed and prayed for three things.

For strength.

For salvation.

And for forgiveness, because I knew my plan was based on lies. I had told my parents I was helping more so that they wouldn't have as many jobs to do.

But they seemed grateful and as a reward they gave me a set amount of money to spend if I wanted to go out. I continued going to the disco with Lucy every week. I deliberately only used enough money for bus fares and the entrance fee so that I would have money left to go an extra night too. I never bought drinks while I was out, or sweets, as this would have been frivolous.

My money was my escape.

My way out.

My 'get out of jail free' card.

Each night I was lucky enough to have money to go to the disco and escape Bill's visits, I silently rejoiced, grateful for every precious second I was away from him. A little bit more of me had become liberated back into the waiting world, allowing me to spread my clipped wings a little further each time. I had been given a little of my jail sentence back.

Twelve

IT WAS AT the disco one Friday that I met a boy called Daniel. Lucy didn't like him very much but I did – he was polite and fairly quiet. Lucy's favourites were the better-looking boys who all the other girls went for.

Daniel was really quite sweet. Although he wasn't very tall and was a bit cuddly, he had a warm smile that instantly made you feel happy. He was considerate and he had lovely brown eyes – eyes that would smile kindly at me each time I saw him. Daniel helped out at the disco and went to the church there on Sundays. I hadn't seen him before because he had been away on holiday, and I found out after talking with him that he was a lot older than me. It didn't seem to matter much about the four-year age gap. We got on well together, he was a good listener and he treated me as if I was really special. Daniel was quite shy, but he plucked up courage to ask me out. He took me home that night in his car. Not only was he older, but he had his own car too!

We agreed to meet on the following Sunday afternoon. I hadn't been this happy since Tom had left. Little did I know when I walked through the door that my world was about to take another hard knock.

Dad wasn't pleased that a boy old enough to drive had dropped me off. He was angry and I could tell. He asked me lots of questions when I came in about Dan before he would allow me to go to bed. I was up for what seemed like hours being interrogated, but I couldn't understand why he was so upset. He finished by telling me older boys didn't hang around with girls my age unless they were after something. I knew only too well what he meant.

I went to bed that night upset and annoyed. How dare he tell me boys are only after one thing? Hadn't he already taken that thing from me? What else was left? Who had been watching out for me then, when he came calling at my bedroom door? Who was there to protect me from *his* grasp?

I fell into a restless sleep, and dreamed that night

about a life with Daniel. He was my salvation and my hope, although he didn't know it yet. It seemed that someone was trying to help me.

But Bill also visited my dreams that night, reminding me of his warning to remain quiet about what had happened.

I woke up in a cold sweat; all Dan's warmth had long since gone.

I became more determined than ever that night as I tried to go back to sleep. I *was* going to make it in my fight for survival. I liked Daniel, and no one was going to make me stop seeing him or get in the way of our newfound happiness. Not even my dad.

I saw Daniel lots of times after that. In fact, I saw him rather more than I should have done. He took me to the disco every night it was open, and we spent a lot of time together at weekends. He also introduced me to stock-car racing. I loved it. It was great fun watching the cars getting smashed up as they raced around, and feeling the blasts of the air horns of enthusiasts all around me gave me a real buzz. It was just so exciting, and it was in these moments that I found a wider corridor to escape down, a corridor where the doors were never locked.

Mum told me that Bill had called up at the house

a few times over the week, but as it was the school holidays she had told him I was out with Daniel. I saw Bill one evening passing the cemetery as we drove in the other direction. He was going to the house. I breathed a sigh of relief that I wouldn't be there. He would not be able to capture me. Not tonight, at least …

He didn't see me in Daniel's car. I was glad, because it meant he didn't know what to look out for. Inside my mind, I felt as if I were a convict on the run, even though I knew now more than ever that what was happening to me, what Bill was doing to me, was not my fault.

I enjoyed being with Daniel; he was like a breath of fresh air. We started going out in a foursome with his friend Paul and his girlfriend Karina. We were all great friends. And slowly I began to fall in love with Daniel, in the same way that I knew he already loved me.

The last big stock-car meeting of the season was being held in Blackpool at the Norbreck Castle Hotel. We all went to the meeting – it was a lovely hot day and I had a wonderful time. We ate hot dogs, drank pop and for a few short hours I actually let go of my troubled thoughts. I closed the lid on the bad-memories box that had been stored deep in my mind, and I allowed myself to drift into a world I should have known so well.

Daniel had shown me this new world.

Daniel had set me free.

He had helped me in the same way Tom had.

I didn't want that day to end. When we arrived home, we sat close together, holding each other, enjoying our cuddle. We kissed for a long time sitting outside the house, warm and snug in his little white Mini with its shiny black roof. I noticed it had become cold outside – summer was drawing to a close – but inside the car we felt so cosy together. I didn't want this moment to end. I knew I was falling in love with Dan.

That night Dan told me he loved me.

I was truly happy for the first time since Tom had left.

It was a happiness I knew I didn't deserve.

I had been so bad.

I had done terrible things.

I had let old men do terrible things to me.

I had lied to my mum.

I had told so many lies.

And lying, I knew, was a sin.

I should have stayed happy that night, cradled in the love and warmth that Daniel was offering me; but instead an uninviting, haunting coldness fell around me. A coldness that kept me in a dark shadow.

I tried to sleep, but sleep never stood a chance against the battle of memories that had begun to erupt inside my head. I tossed and turned deep into the night. In the end, my eyes fell wearily shut as the sun broke through the gap in the curtains.

Mum woke me at eleven o'clock. 'Wake up, sleepyhead,' her voice echoed around the room. 'Bill's here for you.'

Please, no, let it be a dream. He can't be back.

Can he?

The tears welled quickly beneath my closed eyelids. As I pulled my legs free from the bedclothes, I fell to the floor. I lay there tangled up in sheets, shock and a sleepy unconsciousness. What was he doing here? It was the middle of the day. Why wasn't he at the bingo hall? What did he want?

It wasn't his day!

What gave him the right continually to think he was entitled to any more days with me? These days that belonged to me. This was now my life. I was starting to take control, and he was not welcome.

Inside, I felt an overwhelming anger gripping me, an anger that I had never felt before. I wanted my life back. I wanted to be me again. I wanted to become the girl I should have been. I knew he had come on a different day because I had succeeded in loosening his chains over the past week – something I knew angered him deeply. I knew he wasn't happy with how things were, with the way I had started to treat him. He resented what I was doing and I knew it.

When I went slowly, sleepily down the stairs, I heard voices travelling through the kitchen from the lounge. Mum's voice was muffled, making it hard for me to tell what she was saying, but his voice was perfectly understandable. He spoke in lower tones than he usually did, but the insistent nature of his questioning sounded even more desperate with every word he spoke. 'When did she meet him? How old is he? And you're letting her go out with him, Evelyn, with such a big age difference? You'll have to be careful. What will people think?' He barely gave Mum a chance to answer.

He had a cheek. What right had he to question my mum about Dan? Who did he think he was? I walked into the room and stared at him angrily. I guessed at that moment that he knew exactly what I was thinking. He glared at me. In the glare of his eye I could see hatred shining through, hatred and glistening resentment.

Why did he have this look? What gave him the right to look at me in this way? What had I done wrong?

I hated him more than ever. All I wanted to do was escape forever.

I wished Dan were there.

Within half an hour, I was sitting in his car again, travelling the same old familiar roads. There weren't any ways now to his flat I didn't know. I had memorised them all. I was trapped and heading for the flat. Mum had once more sent me with him.

I had objected. He had objected to my objecting. He had said Mum had promised I would help him today. And twenty-five minutes later we were driving down his street. He pulled the car to a halt. 'OK,' he said, 'come on, out you get.'

He was treating me like a criminal. He looked at me so strongly I felt myself shrink in fear, my whole body sinking into the seat I was sitting on. I didn't move for a few moments. I couldn't. Fear held me firm. 'Come on,' he hissed through clenched teeth as he grabbed my wrist and pulled me across the seat towards him.

I had no alternative. I had to get out of the car. My wrist felt terribly bruised and swollen. He held on to me as he opened the door and climbed the stairs up

124

to the first-floor landing, through the door and into his flat. I pulled free of him at last; he retaliated by pushing me on to the chair. 'What do you think you are doing, going out with that lad?'

'Is that any of your business?' I shouted back at him.

I recoiled in shock at the words I had spoken; the voice I had heard didn't seem to belong to me. It belonged to someone who was strong, alive, someone who knew how to get what she wanted. I had never shouted at or questioned an adult before, and I knew I shouldn't have done it – even in this situation. I glanced at him quickly. Luckily, he had not noticed me falter.

'You know I don't want you going out with boys. They're only after one thing.'

What he really meant was he couldn't bear the thought of anyone else touching me. I'm sure he believed that every touch that wasn't his would poison his precious Sarah, taint her skin so that she would not be wholly his. Bill had built me into his world, a possession he kept caged and imprisoned. I was his. I know he believed I would always be his.

Over the last few precious days, the chains that had bound me had loosened. For that short period of time I had actually believed I could get away from him. How wrong I was. The chains were back — I knew that the moment he pulled me to him, pushed me on to the bed and did all the things he had done so many times before to me. The difference was that this time he did those things with a forceful, hurtful, menacing fixation. And he continued to do them regardless of my pleas to stop, which continuously rang out in the hours that followed.

He hurt me that day — really hurt me. I pulled away from him several times. Each time he overpowered me. He pulled me back, trapping me beneath him like a small frail bird under a bold eagle. He got what he wanted. He made me regret my actions.

He pushed and poked into me even harder.

He acted like this was his only purpose in life.

I was his property, and all I had to do was remember that.

I hurt for days after. I felt as if he had torn into every small, intimate part of me, ripping me apart with every move he made. The bruises on my thighs lasted forever, like the memories he had already created. I saw them in the mirror that afternoon. Each day they became clearer than they had been the day before, their intensity crying out to me as I looked at my battered, bruised body. Those bruises reminded me of him. Of the minutes that lasted longer than an hour, minutes spent with a vile, wicked, hateful monster.

The bruises faded in time, but the feeling of being held against my will stayed deep in my mind, penetrating my subconscious with the same intensity that Bill had used on me. I had the memory of his hands feeling me and pawing me bubbling in my mind like a spa that was never turned off. I finally understood that he had been raping me. He had been taking me to his flat against my will, holding me down against my will, and penetrating me against my will.

Dan came to see me that night. He wanted to go out for a drive, but I told him I wasn't well. I lied. I couldn't have gone out with him, even if I had wanted to. Dad wouldn't let me use the hot water for a bath that afternoon; he wanted me to have one later when Mum had done her washing. I felt worthless and dirty. I didn't want Dan to hold me until I had scrubbed that feeling of worthlessness away, along with *his* presence, his scent, his touch.

Bill had made me feel like an inconsequential person, a person who had no life left and nothing to live for. I tried not to think about him or what he had done to me while I patiently waited for the three hours to pass before I would be allowed to have a bath. Every second his scent remained on me I become more and more alone.

All the time I waited, listening to each long minute tick by, my body felt more sordid and repulsive. I wanted to change everything I could see. I even wondered how I could get new skin, then it wouldn't matter about washing the old one. I knew I was dreaming my life into a fantasy world that did not exist; but if you can't dream you have nothing.

I began thinking back to the plans I had made in my head. I decided I would push things forward. I thought about Dan and how I felt about him. I knew I didn't want to be alone without him. He made me feel loved and wanted. He had shown me a new, caring world I could take part in. He had given me back my worth in the way he treated me, and he had shared his strength with me. But I knew that Bill would destroy him the same way that he would have devastated Tom. I knew Dan must never know, never find out.

I pledged to take this secret to the grave, vowing that neither of them would ever know the truth about their Sarah …

Thirteen

I PLANNED LONG into the days that followed. I had to do something quickly. Just when I thought I was safe again Bill had turned up without warning, and he did it twice more that very week. He spoke to Mum and, as usual, he got his way. I vaguely heard the conversation between the two of them taking shape. Mum's voice was more audible than Bill's this time: 'Yes, she can go and help you. No, she doesn't have anything planned. Of course she could see Daniel tomorrow.' That afternoon I had to go with Bill no matter how much I complained.

After that moment, I again swore to myself that I would try to protect myself. I vowed he would not violate me again, ever. I had to break his binding chains. Chains that I knew he had locked all too securely. I knew I had to examine them more closely. There had to be a weakness in the links somewhere. I had to find a way, any way, to break free. I knew Bill wouldn't be happy if he suspected what I was planning, and I also knew in my head he would do everything in his power to stop me setting myself free of him. He would find a way to make the chains stronger if I gave him the chance.

I had to think faster, become smarter, and stay one step ahead.

I wasn't sure if my original plans would work now he knew I was avoiding him. That night I prayed hard in bed, begging someone, anyone, whoever and wherever they were, to answer me. I wanted someone to open their ears wider, to listen out for my cry for help. Surely someone somewhere had to be paying attention.

I decided to try something I hadn't tried before. I went through the scenario, step by step, in my mind. It was a simple thing, but to me it seemed the most difficult thing in the world: when Bill next came, I would just say no to him.

'No, I'm not coming with you today.'

I said the words over and over in my head.

'No, I'm not coming with you today.'

'No, I'm not coming with you today.'

'No, I'm not coming with you today.'

'No, I'm not coming with you today.'

Each time I spoke the words, they sounded louder, more positive. But when I heard his car pull up outside the house the following day, they became quieter, and I stumbled over them.

I was scared.

How does a small person stand tall in the face of such overwhelming danger?

I heard his car door close. The gate opened and creaked slowly shut after him, sounding louder than it ever had before. A few moments later I heard his silly tap on the door – a feeble tap that belonged to a feeble man. The door opened and his footsteps pattered their way across the kitchen floor. 'It's only me,' his voice rang out.

Inside my head, I answered his call. 'If it's only you, *go away*!' I wished more than anything that I had the courage actually to say it to his face, but I hadn't. I couldn't. I shouldn't.

But why shouldn't I? He was the one who was doing wrong. But it wasn't allowed to yell or shout at adults. Children had to know their place, after all. Answering back just wasn't something I would do.

Mum's voice sounded out in the distance – she was

on her way in from the back garden. She greeted him with her usual 'hello', and asked if he wanted a cup of tea.

'No thanks,' I heard him reply. 'I only came to pick up Sarah.'

Inside, my body shook with disbelief. I wanted to hear him say to her that he was taking me with him to abuse me. I wanted him to tell the truth and break this unbelievable, elongated spell of lying. I wanted to hear him say to her that for the past three years he had been abusing me. I wanted to hear him say sorry.

A few minutes passed. I heard muffled sounds drifting up the stairs from the room below. I knew Mum would call me any second, but I was shocked when she hadn't called me ten minutes later. I couldn't stand the apprehensive wait. I walked slowly down the stairs, shaking with fear; Mum opened the door just as I reached for the handle. I jumped because I hadn't expected that to happen. Bill was getting up from the chair behind her. He smiled the smile I hated. This time I smiled back. He was totally unprepared for what happened next.

'Are you right?' he said. 'We'd better go'

I watched him fumble for his keys in his pocket as he headed towards the door. I saw a look of glee in his eyes, delight written into his creased face. I knew what he was expecting to happen more than anyone: a short drive to the flat, where he would wash me, have sex with me, ejaculate over me and discard me.

Not this bloody time, mate … I was finally going to take charge of my destiny.

'Sorry,' I replied, 'I can't today. Lucy is on her way over. We've got a test to study for.'

I slowly looked up at him. He had already figured out the truth – I could tell from the glint of fuming anger that I saw reflected in the light that caught each of his eyes as he turned to face me. I stared back in such a way that I hope said, 'Not any more. No way. You're finished.'

He just turned towards the door. As he left, he said, 'See you Friday then.'

Little did he realise I would be waiting, ready again with my newfound strength.

The door shut, the gate creaked and whined after him, the car door thudded and the engine hummed less and less as he got closer and closer to the end of the street. And with each passing second I felt my freedom grow. This time it was being watered by hope.

I walked to the outhouse, found the oil and gently put some on the gate hinges. It silently closed into place. If I didn't know better, I'd have sworn I heard a thank you making its way from the hinges to my ears.

Later that night I saw Daniel. I never felt happier than I did the moment his little Mini pulled up outside the front gate. We went for a drive and then down to the church hall to move some boxes for the vicar. Daniel sensed I was happier, more at ease than usual. He told me he felt there was something different about me but he didn't know what it was. I just giggled at him. We had a great night, talking and laughing – laughter that seemed to be laughed more freely somehow. Daniel held me close to him that night. I felt him press against me. Inside, my heart was missing beats and my tummy felt as if it were floating away. That night our bodies entwined and became one. I wanted what I felt with Daniel to last forever: security, love and warmth within his arms and within his heart.

But I knew I had to face reality. My dreaming stopped the moment Daniel drove me home that night. I tried to sleep but I couldn't. I understood what I had planned to do to keep Bill at bay had made him furious. I knew he was more annoyed than ever. I planned to be out when he called on Friday – that way I would well and truly avoid him. I called to see Lucy the morning after and arranged a visit to town.

I wasn't quite prepared for what happened when he turned up on Thursday.

I had been busy revising for tests at school. Mock exams were looming and I so desperately wanted to do well in them. It was English Literature first. I loved the subject but I always seemed to struggle to remember the things I had read. I was frantically reading one of the set books when, at about half past six, Bill appeared. Mum had gone to the shop and Dad was busy decorating the kitchen.

Bill had let himself in through the back door, and he spent twenty minutes or so talking to Dad. I stopped revising; I couldn't concentrate now. He was back and I couldn't hear what was being said in the kitchen below. My concentration had gone and fear was creeping into its place. I was frightened knowing that I had to try yet again to escape him. I wasn't even safe here, in my own home. He was everywhere – I felt as if he were stalking me. He was always there, if not physically then mentally, in my every waking moment. I felt caged and trapped with no escape route available.

I heard the hall door open, then Dad called upstairs to me. 'Bill's here, Sarah.'

I wanted to curl up and go to sleep, to find myself waking up from the dream.

Dad shouted at me again, impatience sounding in every word. 'Sarah, Bill's here!'

I went down.

'Bill's come round. He needs help in the snack bar – Jean isn't there, she's unwell today. I said I knew you'd want to help out in any way you could.' He smiled at me as he finished what he was saying.

'I have to revise; I have an exam to get through next week.'

'Oh, there's plenty of time for that, you have all weekend,' Dad replied.

'We won't be gone long,' Bill added, as if to secure the deal with Dad.

I thought for a moment then continued with my protest. 'I can't go. I'm sorry, but I have to revise.' The quiver in my voice broke free with the last few words I spoke. 'This exam is really important to me, Dad. You want me to do well, don't you?'

They both looked at each other, then they directed their attention towards me. Dad looked angry. He was angry that I was backchatting him. Bill was looking at me with eyes that seemed to be burning through me as fast as any acid could have done. I felt so uncomfortable. I hated standing here having Bill's eyes bore fiercely into me. Dad didn't help matters either, siding with everything Bill said. I felt like any naughty child would have done, in trouble for taking a biscuit without asking or eating sweets too close to teatime

No matter how much I objected, Dad still insisted I go. I took my time going to the loo before leaving, combing my hair three times, washing my face four. That way there wouldn't be lots of time at the flat. All the time I dawdled I realised what I was actually doing was attempting to take back some of the minutes Bill wanted to steal from me. All the minutes I was in the car, moving along the streets heading towards the flat, I wanted to jump out to escape him. My feelings about what was happening to me had changed over the past weeks. I felt different about myself. New thoughts and feelings had grown inside of me, making me feel more anxious with each passing day. I had begun to feel like a cheap prostitute again, cheap yet exclusive to him. After all, hadn't I been the best kind of girl for a man of his age – untouched and untried by anyone else before him. Rich new pickings. Unblemished. Brought slowly into new awakenings within my body by him and him alone. And, best of all, I was completely free.

Back at his flat, he spent longer looking at me than he normally did, looking at how my body had changed. He had tried to take all my clothes off but I made so much fuss and wriggled so wildly he gave up in the end. I would not lie under the covers with him or get into bed with him without my clothes on, which was what he had expected me to do willingly that day. This really annoyed him. He wanted to see me climb into bed with him in the same joyful way as young lovers would have done. It was his sick, sordid, soiled way of thinking. After all, he reminded me, it wasn't as if he had never seen my breasts and vagina before.

That night after getting home I managed to get into the bathroom first. I heard Mum shouting, annoyance sounding out in her voice that someone had used all the hot water, but I didn't care any more about her, Dad or anyone else.

I had had my bath. I had earned it. I scrubbed harder than ever, my skin becoming extremely tender and sore. I had to wash his persistent handprints off me. I had to remove his soiled stains. I used Mum's scrubbing brush and the Vim. I looked in the mirror when I had finished, but underneath the red, swollen scratches I'd made with the brush, I could still see handprints, as if they were indelible.

Fourteen

AFTER THAT DAY, Bill didn't call as often. I went out and enjoyed myself and did what other teenagers did. It felt quite strange at first. I went to the disco more often, shared time with my friends and I saw lots more of Daniel. During this time we went to more stock-car meetings. I particularly enjoyed going on the thirty-mile journey to Bolton because it meant being away from home for longer.

I loved travelling to other towns. I loved every moment alone in Dan's Mini, in our own special world, a world that had no space for Bill in it. Daniel and I became even closer and shared lots of time together. But I always felt as if I had deceived and tricked him in some way. Even when I was happy I felt I had let him down. I often used to go off into my own little dream world and spend time thinking about how he would have felt if he had known his girlfriend, whom he thought so much of, had been the regular plaything of a sixty-one-year-old paedophile.

I think that Daniel – as loving and gentle as he was – would not have been able to cope with my past. I know he would never have intentionally hurt me, but I recognised deep inside my heart that he would not have been able to help, or protect himself from, the feelings of bitterness and hatred that would have overflowed from his heart into his mind, in time destroying what we had carefully built together.

It's a terrible thing to think about abuse, let alone come to terms with it.

Daniel and I had been going out with each other for five months when things began to change. He had wanted me to go to an important stock-car meeting with him, but he forgot to tell me about it. He called on the off-chance that Dad would let me go out with him, but Dad had never let me go out in the week unless he knew about it in advance. When Daniel arrived I was delighted to see him, but Dad was in one of his usual bad moods. I knew it was a desperate situation. Dad came into the kitchen, saw Daniel and immediately walked out of the room again. He called me into the lounge. Dad disliked Daniel, as he had the first time he saw him. He hated the age gap. In fact, he hated me being with boys full stop.

He asked me why Daniel was here, and once I told him about the meeting and wanting to go out the same night, he was even angrier. I had no idea what had got into him but he took his anger out on Daniel. He walked into the kitchen, asking him all kinds of questions. 'Why do you want to go out with Sarah? Do you know how old she is?' Dad had always suspected me of lying to Daniel about my age; he never really understood Daniel or me.

'Yes, I do know how old she is, she's fourteen,' Daniel replied as he moved closer to me.

Dad looked even more annoyed when he saw Daniel take my hand. It seemed to fuel his anger even more than before. 'Well, you may as well go home,' he snarled at him. 'She will *not* be coming out tonight.'

Daniel looked hurt and upset. Dad had behaved badly and I could tell by the look in Daniel's eyes that he was getting fed up of his ever-worsening attitude towards him. He walked out of the house and made his way to the car. I followed him. I needed to talk to him so badly, alone and away from Dad. I got into the car with Daniel and we sat talking outside the house for the next hour. All the time I was there, Dad kept calling me in from the window.

Daniel had been my lifeline, my hope and inspiration in the weeks that had passed. He had fended off the stalker in my life just by being there, yet he was unaware of Bill's existence and what he had done to me. Now he was slipping away from me, and who could blame him? The age difference had never been a problem, but now it was different – Daniel was being punished by Dad's assault of words, words that he didn't deserve. His only crime had been loving me and wanting me. I knew how upset he was at being treated like a schoolboy, but I was on my own – Mum wouldn't help for fear of reprisal and another argument flaring up between them both. She knew how bad Dad could be and, not unnaturally, she wanted to keep on his best side.

I once asked Dad why he had treated Daniel so badly but he just pushed me aside as he left the room, refusing to answer my question.

Our friend Karina knew Daniel was fed up and had taken to talking to him whenever she got the chance. She was a year older than me and was still going out with Paul. We saw them occasionally, but we didn't go out as a group like we used to do. Karina had become quite fond of Daniel, and she didn't hide the fact. She flirted with him and, one day, when I saw them together, I realised I was losing him. I watched Daniel with Karina the following week and felt so alone. I wanted to move away, go somewhere else where it would be just the two of us. I knew from the way he had begun to look at her that he was going to leave me and go to her. The pain I felt that night was insufferable. I felt as if my whole body had once more become crushed and trapped by sadness.

Dan and I parted as friends, but I felt more alone than ever. I had lost my renewed hope and faith all in one. The bright light that had shone on Daniel and me, bringing hope with it, had become a flickering, faltering candle, running out of both wax and wick; a candle placed by an open window waiting cautiously for the next gust of wind to extinguish it.

What was I to do?

Who could I turn to for salvation now?

Who would help me?

I felt so alone.

So troubled.

So afraid.

And so very, very desperate.

It had been three weeks since Daniel and I had split up. I seemed to have lost my energy and that newfound enthusiasm for life. My passion for living had walked out on me. I felt lonely. I certainly couldn't talk to Karina. She had taken my place. The only true friend I ever had had been stolen by another so-called friend. I never really fathomed out why she had to do this to me. It was yet another blow to my confidence. The once bright light that Daniel had illuminated in my heart had been extinguished.

My life started to grind to a halt. Even Lucy wasn't available to chat any more. Her time was taken up pursuing a boy called Adam. She was head over heels about him. Totally besotted. But he was two years older than her and didn't even notice her – not the way she wanted him to. We used to get off the bus after the disco and once he was around the street corner we would follow him just so Lucy could spend longer looking at him, often through his kitchen window once he had returned home. She had it bad.

Adam was a nice boy, so who could blame her. I knew what she saw in him and why she wanted to go out with him so badly. Adam wasn't very tall, but he was blond and handsome with the most amazing blue eyes. Eyes that were both welcoming and appealing. I used to say that eyes like his were 'go to bed' eyes. I didn't really understand what I was saying way back then, but now I know what the words mean I realise how true they were. He truly had beautiful, inviting eyes, eyes that were surrounded with love, a love that was ready to be shared.

And my time had been taken up with other things, too. I had been seeing Paul since he had asked me out a couple of weeks previously. He was a good laugh, but sometimes he was a little too serious. We had spent quite a bit of time together and we seemed to be becoming close. We saw each other at the disco, where Dan still went with Karina.

One day, Bill appeared as if by magic. No one said he was coming. No one said anything when he appeared at the door. It was as if he had slipped into place as part of the family. He walked into the room, grinning. I had always hated the way he had assumed such familiarity within my home. He walked in as if he had always been here. Every room downstairs within his reach had become tainted and discoloured by his very presence. He brought foul air into the kitchen, a sour, bitter smell that old perverted men have with them, an odour that they can't get rid of but to people like me, people who have been abused and taken advantage of, it is an odour you can't mistake.

He sat around for the next forty minutes grinning at me, each five minutes that ticked by seemed like five hours. Then he looked at his watch, stood up and said he should be off as he had sandwiches to prepare. I moved uncomfortably in my seat and felt my blood run cold when I heard the words that left Mum's mouth: 'If you hang on a minute, Sarah will come and help you.'

He glanced at her, looked at me and smiled his pathetic smile. He looked as if he had won a jackpot prize at the bingo. I remember clearly how vigorously I objected, but she would have none of it. I had to go and that was that. I looked across to where Dad was sitting: he smiled at Bill and avoided my gaze.

No, surely not …

I had to be wrong …

Were they in it together now?

Were they going to compare notes when Bill brought me home?

Dad would never do that. Would he?

Bill once again took me to his flat to do as he wished. He did all his usual things. I lay there rigid, weeping, begging him now more than ever to stop.

He said he enjoyed being with me. He thought I was beautiful and he always wanted to be able to visit me.

I wanted him to stop so desperately. I jumped away from him before he ejaculated all over my tummy. I gained fresh courage that afternoon; where it came from I don't think I will ever know. I just knew that this had to end. If it didn't, then next time I would end my life successfully, without any goodbyes to get in my way or rescue me.

I remember somewhere along the journey home becoming very calm. I think it was shock, mainly – the shock of realising I had gained some strength. As we drew up outside the house, I told Bill that that was the last time I would ever go with him.

He looked at me fiercely, but this time I felt cool. I told him that I wanted to be with my friends and not spend time with him. I told him that I now knew what he was doing was not right. It had taken me almost four years to stand up for my rights as a child; unfortunately, it was too late for me to rescue my childhood back. After all, what point would there be in telling anyone now about a stolen life that could never be recovered and made whole again?

When I finished speaking, he looked at me and grinned. I knew he had not realised I was strong enough to stop him.

Fifteen

AS THE DAYS that followed slipped quietly by, Bill appeared to be keeping his distance from both Mum and me. On the odd occasion Mum went off to bingo, she always asked me to go, but I never did. I didn't want to think about what would happen if I saw Bill, or what he would do if he got a second chance. I knew he would try his best to lie and trap me once more in his odd, perverse world. A world he thought I belonged to.

I still felt fear when his name cropped up in any conversation. I wanted to cry out, shout for help, but I never did. As always I remained silent and soundless. I still had his words from the past firmly fixed in my head: 'No one will believe you.'

As I whispered each one of the words quietly to myself they tasted bitter and sour, leaving me feeling nauseous once more.

Even though Bill wasn't around as much as he had been, I still felt his presence. It was as if he had become entwined with me over the past years, becoming one with my shadow. A limpet on a rock.

I thought long and hard about everything that had happened to me as I lay in bed at night, watching the garden shadows forming mysterious unfamiliar shapes on the bedroom walls. I thought about the situation I was in and the help I should have had.

Why had it taken me so long to build up the strength I needed to free myself from him? I felt as if I had lived my life trapped in his shadow; but unlike the unfamiliar shadows I saw forming on the wall at night, Bill's shadow had a haunting, memorable shape that I would never easily forget. My first memories of his abuse had been locked inside my head for such a long time, packed rapidly away in their box, a box that now was so full it was struggling to stay upright. I had to remove those memories before they weighed me down. If I emptied my box into the river, the memories would sink, drowning them completely, like the men who had come and abused me had each in turn drowned me with their weight.

For over four years, I had wanted to remain a child growing at the right pace, but I couldn't. They would never let me. They each had a plan for me, which they carried out with menacing success until they had their way.

I came to the conclusion that I could never recapture the past; only the future was standing untouched in front of me now. It was up to me to change the course in which I was heading. I had to change it beyond recognition, moving it in a better direction far away from all the troubles and torments that had gone before.

I knew what I had to do, but the question of how left me weeping for hours.

In my heart, the words of my plan unfolded, words that were to be my arrows, arrows that would hopefully keep Bill at bay.

Unusually, Bill stayed away for the rest of that week and part way into the next. I had found myself strangely wanting him to call – a feeling I struggled with and couldn't understand, until I realised that it was linked to my plan to rid myself of him once and for all. I knew that if he didn't come I could not put my plan into action. I continued to have sleepless nights, tossing, turning and dreaming the dreams that had freed the memories, unlocking them from the box in the still of the night. I despised my dreams; in each one I relived my humiliation with feelings of hate and disgust one hundred times over. Each dream was like a painting that had excellent detail and fine clarity. Each day Bill didn't appear during the daytime, my vivid, violent dreams visited me at night, taking his place.

Then, without warning, he came. Smug, sanctimonious, self-righteous and expectant. He was expecting me to be his plaything, a thing to amuse himself with. He was in for a shock.

Bill walked into the kitchen through the unlocked back door, whistling as he moved forward. He stood leaning against the sink, looking around, and every once in a while glancing my way, winking when he thought no one would notice. Each time he did I averted my eyes, my skin feeling as if a thousand millipedes had crawled under it. I felt cheap and soiled before he even had a chance to touch me. He stood there like he owned me.

He asked if it would be OK if I went to help with the sandwiches. Dad looked at him, glanced at me and hesitated for a while. I thought for a moment that he was going to stop what he knew was happening to me, but he didn't. He looked at me again for a brief second then turned to Bill and agreed. I looked across at him as I went out to the car, following Bill slowly. Why hadn't he stopped this? He knew what was happening, yet he stood and did nothing. Was he really my dad, or was he my agent? I wanted to kick and scream from the tallest building, pointing the accusing finger at my abuser first and my father second. But I knew it would serve no purpose. I would be judged and they would be forgiven. After all, grown-ups don't lie, do they?

I sat quietly in the car, not taking part in his conversation. He continued to speak his words, but it was just meaningless rubbish. I had planned this so carefully, I had to act it out meticulously. It had to be right to work. I continued to listen, but continued to say nothing in return.

As the car drew up outside the flat, he got out. I got out too, but took longer than I usually did. Once in the building I ambled along behind him. He sighed a few times as we went up the stairs – I knew that I was annoying him but my heart leaped with wondrous delight each time I heard him sigh. Once in the flat, he took off his coat and kicked off his shoes. I sat by the fire. He looked at me before going into the kitchen for his usual bowl of water. I said nothing but continued to watch him in silence. He came back into the room and left the bowl beside the bed, then he moved towards me.

I stood up fast.

It made him jump. He stepped back momentarily, wondering what was going on. My heart leaped again.

He stood in front of me, looking shocked by my sudden movement. I started to speak, but nerves got the better of me. No words left my mouth. Don't desert me now, I pleaded silently …

He took hold of my hand; I pulled away sharply. He looked at me in the way he had before when he hadn't got what he wanted. It was a look of pure and extreme dislike. He took hold of my hand again. I pulled away from him again.

'What's going on, Sarah?' he asked sharply.

'I don't want you to do this any … any more.' My words fell over each other as I tried to stay in control. 'I don't want you to do this any more. I have a life I'm not living, a life that should have laughter and friends and excitement in it. I am fourteen years old, not forty. I want to be me again, not a toy for you.'

He stood looking at me. 'I thought you enjoyed coming with me. Don't you want to have other things? I could give you money. You'd like that – you'll be able to go and buy new clothes and other things you want. I'll give you five pounds today …'

His reply stunned me and made me catch my breath. He looked at me as his words hit me like a bolt of lightning. Who did he think he was? Was that all he thought I was worth?

'I thought you liked it,' he whispered.

How could I possibly like being abused by this old, sad, crumpled man? How could he possibly think I'd like being abused by any man? What kind of sick, perverted world did he think he lived in? Why did he think I'd want to be a part of that world?

I thought for a moment before I replied. 'I don't want to be here. *I don't like it.* I hate it and I hate you. I hate everything about you. I have for a long time. Each time you've touched me, every second you've touched me I have felt like dirt trampled on the ground beneath everyone's shoes.'

I continued talking slowly so that all my words would register in his ears. 'What reason do you possibly think I could have for staying here, letting you do the things you've done, when out there is a world you have taken from me, a world I want to be part of again before you steal the rest of my life?'

He fell back on to the chair at the side of me, looking shocked by my words. I knew he wasn't expecting me to say such things to him. After all, he was the adult. I was still the child.

'I want you to stay with me, Sarah. That boy doesn't want you; he's just using you …'

'And you aren't?'

'I want you to be here with me more often. I missed you. Can't I still see you on the days when you don't see Paul? I'll share you, I don't mind'.

'You don't understand, do you? I'm older now. I want you to set me free. I don't want to be anywhere near you. I want to be left alone to follow the path *I* want to follow, not the path you've set out for me. I want to go my own way; I want to be with people my own age. I'm missing my life because you've taken it from me. You continually steal precious minutes from me, my minutes, minutes that aren't yours to take.'

I looked at him. He was ready to speak but I had to finish what I'd started. 'I want it back before it's too late,' I added hesitantly.

I waited for his reply. My heart was racing – the beats felt like a bass drum beating louder than ever inside of me. He looked at me and replied, but this time I could hear the mounting venom in his voice as he spoke the words. 'I think you are being ungrateful. You are not being fair. I've tried to take you away from your life on that council estate, tried to make things better for you by showing you there are other things outside of there.'

I was traumatised by his accusing words: did he really expect me to be grateful for the abuse he had subjected me to? 'Other things? The only other things you have shown me are the four walls of this flat, and the sand hills in Blackpool. I want you to leave me alone. I am still a growing child. I am not an adult. I won't let you do this to me any more, Bill.'

I stood still for a moment, watching his reaction to my last few words – they had left my mouth quicker and with more power than I expected.

Then he spoke. 'How will you stop me?'

'I'll go to the police and tell them everything. Today.'

'Don't be stupid. They won't believe you.'

'I think you'll find that they'll listen. After all, how many times has that lady downstairs seen you bringing me here?'

As he looked at me, he seemed to be getting smaller; shrivelling up into the insignificant old man he was. He didn't look like a man in control any more. He looked as if he had lost everything he had.

Had I won? Was that my trump card, or did he have an ace up his sleeve?

I looked at him, watched him as he got up and slowly put his shoes on, waiting apprehensively for his next word. He said nothing. He just beckoned me to follow him out of the flat. As he drove the car away from the flat that night, he took a longer route home. I didn't know where I was and all I could do was sit still and wait for the familiar streets to return. If he changed direction in the past I would usually ask him where we were going. Tonight I didn't. I didn't want him to know I was worried about what he was doing. He would have enjoyed that.

Fifty minutes later I was home. He grabbed hold of me before I could open the car door. 'You'll regret this, Sarah, you know you will.'

'No I won't. I never will. But you might, one day.'

I stood outside the back door for a few minutes before I went in, trying to control my violently shaking body. Eventually I wiped my damp eyes and slowly opened the kitchen door. I went inside. Mum looked beyond me into the hall, looking for Bill. 'He's not coming in tonight, Mum. He's had to go off somewhere. He said he'd see you at bingo,' I lied.

At least she didn't question me any further. I was relieved – if she had done, I think I would probably have opened up and told her everything that had happened. She continued sorting out the cutlery and plates ready for tea. 'OK, love. Tea's ready.'

I slept easier that night after my bath. I threw my

clothes away that I had worn that day. The important thing was I had to have a clean start, a start without the soiled images in that open box of bad memories. As I slept, I dreamed of closing the lid. I wanted to push it out of my mind, but it was too heavy, fixed tightly in place. The only thing I could do was close the lid firmly now that I didn't need it any more.

Sixteen

IN THE YEAR that followed, lots of things happened to me. I went out more, and spent more time with Paul. I began to enjoy what was left of my stolen adolescence because I knew it was the only thing left I could rescue. My childhood years had already gone forever, never to be retrieved. What I had left I had to make the most of. I had to live life to the full and that was what I intended to do.

No one guided me through, no one showed me the right or wrong path to take; it was just me, on my own, proceeding cautiously. All I could do now was take one step at a time. Then one hour at a time. And finally one day at a time.

I was just trying to live through the traumatic

reminders of my past, trying to put goodness and laughter in places where sadness and tears had ruled for so long. I gradually put aside what had happened to me, although it was never easy. I tried to replace my memories of Bill with good ones of my own, but it wasn't always straightforward, especially when the bad ones still outweighed the good ones. But I progressively replaced each one of those bad memories with those of people that I cared about and loved so sincerely.

I had the memories that Paul gave me. New memories. Good memories. I also had memories that Daniel had left me: these were my bright memories. And I had Tom's memories all stacked high inside my good box. Tom's memories were the ones that I learned to treasure the most: it was him who helped me when I was at my lowest ebb. He understood me the most. The times I spent with Tom were good, precious, wonderful times.

During the time I spent with Paul, I became very close to him, and in 1977, when I was just fifteen, I became pregnant. I was so frightened of what my parents would say. I didn't tell them until I was almost ten weeks pregnant. Mum was furious. 'She can go and get rid of it, she's just too young to be a mother,' she yelled.

'It's my baby. I won't.'

'You will do as you are told, my girl, and that's final.' I watched anger mounting in her face. She was adamant she would get her way. 'Where is he, anyway? Why isn't he here facing the music?'

'He's at work,' I answered. 'He has to work.'

'Well, he'd better not show his face around here again. You are going to get rid of it, Sarah. There is no way you are keeping a baby at fifteen.'

I looked at Mum, and then across the room to where Dad was sitting. 'I am keeping my baby. You can't make me get rid of it. It's my baby and I will be sixteen when he's born.'

Mum was angrier than ever. 'You'll do as I say!'

At that moment, Dad butted into the conversation. He wanted to have his say, but that just made Mum madder. 'If she's sixteen when the baby is born, Evelyn, then she has a right to make her own decision. But I will say this to you, Sarah: you have made your bed so you will lie in it. Don't come crying to us if you can't cope or if things go wrong with Paul. We won't be here to pick up the pieces. It's your decision and you'll live by it. Do you understand?'

'Yes, Dad, I do.'

That evening I walked out of the lounge and away from my parents' support. I heard them discussing me, talking about the financial implications and how they couldn't support me and a child – they just didn't have the money.

The next evening I got a bus into town and met up with Paul. We now had to tell his parents. His mum looked hurt at the news – after all, this was the first time they had met me and they were also being told I was pregnant. His dad was furious and rose from his seat sharply, calling Paul 'a bloody fool'.

'How old are you, girl?' he shouted at me.

I was just about to say fifteen when Paul quickly interrupted. 'She's seventeen.' Why was he lying to his parents? Why hadn't he told the truth? After an uneasy half-hour we left, and as we walked to the bus stop I asked Paul why he had lied about my age.

'I lied because, if I hadn't, my dad would have given me the hiding of my life. He'd have kicked me from one end of the street to the other.' He looked at me with those soppy, deep-brown eyes of his and I swallowed all his lies. It wasn't that his father would have beaten him: it was more that if his dad found out I was only fifteen he would have known his son could have been prosecuted for having sex with a minor.

We sat on the bus that night talking about what we would do. We agreed to stay with our parents until we managed to find a flat to live in. Paul told me it would only be for a few weeks – in the end, it turned out to be five months. During that time, Paul did come to the house, and Dad had a go at him, telling him he was no good for his daughter, but, if he was what I wanted, he had better make damn sure that he supported me well.

The next time Paul visited he said that he couldn't find a flat on the wages he earned so he was thinking of joining the army.

'What about us, the baby?' For the first time since I became pregnant, I doubted Paul's commitment to me.

'You can live with your parents, can't you? And I can send you money each week for the baby.'

'Well, I suppose, if that's what you want …'

'I think it's for the best, Sarah, that way I can support you better.'

I watched him walking off towards the end of the street an hour later that night. He was walking with purpose, his head held high with relief. I wondered if he had just told me of his plans for the army to frighten me and get out of being lumbered with a baby. I half-expected that he wanted to hear the words, 'It's OK, Paul, I don't want to be a burden. Forget me, forget the baby and go and enjoy your life.' I never did say those words because this was his responsibility too. This was his child I was having, he had to be responsible at some time in his life so now was a good time to start.

He didn't visit me for two weeks after that. I thought he had deserted us when one Sunday morning he appeared saying he had found us a flat in Ashley. It was a bed-sit, one large attic room in a good, middle-class area. I loved it, although I wasn't looking forward to climbing the three flights of stairs with a pram.

Once I had moved out of home, I felt differently towards my parents and they behaved differently towards me. When I had told them that Paul had found a flat for us, Mum changed somehow. She suggested I stay at home and live with them. I could go back to school to finish my education. As she continued talking to me, telling me of her plans, I knew that this would never work. I felt that I wouldn't be my baby's mum – my mother would. She would take over, raising my child her way. She told me how she would take him for walks and have him in her and my father's room so that he wouldn't disturb me in the night. It was at that point I knew I would lose him if I stayed home and didn't move in with Paul. I knew they both believed I was too young, but in my heart I had done all the growing up I needed to in order to become a good, caring, considerate mum to my child.

A few nights later, my suitcase packed, I left home. I wasn't yet sixteen. Paul came to collect me and we went to catch the bus together. My dad looked at me caringly as I made my way to the door. He grabbed me, gave me a hug and spoke into my ear. I thought he was going to say sorry for what he had done to me; but the sorry I expected never came. Instead, he told me that, if I ever needed them, or was unsure, all I had to do was say the word and I could come home again. His words and Mum's plans made me even more determined to go it alone. This was now my life, not theirs, and I was determined that I would succeed and overcome whatever was thrown my way.

More importantly, I knew I would never see Bill again after I left home.

Our baby was born six weeks later, a beautiful, fine and healthy boy. We soon moved from the large bed-sit in Ashley to a two-bedroom flat nearer the town.

Before I married Paul, I told him about my past. I thought I was doing the right thing, telling him the truth about the person he was about to marry. It was the hardest thing I had ever done.

Paul and I had some good times together, but things were never really as wonderful as I expected them to be. He never really loved me the way I loved him – something had always been missing. During our second year of marriage, things became difficult and I wanted to leave Paul because he was drinking and spending all our money. I also discovered he had been seeing another woman. One night I told him of my plans to leave him. He threatened to tell the world about my past if I did. I thought he understood, but it turned out he was no better that night than any of the men who had raided me of those perfect childhood years.

I stayed, and gradually things smoothed out. I forgave him for what he had said, but I never stopped believing that he now thought I was responsible for what had happened to me. We eventually split up after seven years, despite managing to have some good times together. My family had also grown too. While I was married to Paul, I gave birth to three more wonderful bundles of joy, three more terrific boys.

As my marriage to Paul was ending, I met the one person who would change my life forever. It was a quarter past six one evening early in November and I was going home to visit my parents. After arriving at the bus station to catch a connecting bus, I was introduced to a friend of Paul's brother. From that moment on he had a huge impact on my life, and, when Paul and I divorced the following year, I started seeing and married this extraordinary person.

In the last nineteen years, he has given me so much. We have even added to our family with the welcome addition of a fifth son. My husband has added warmth, light and laughter into my life. He has shown me love and understanding. He has protected me and kept me safe, and has become an amazing father to our wonderful children.

The abuse I suffered made me very protective of my children. I never let them play on the streets when they were little, and I did everything possible to keep them out of danger. I watched them all the time. I was aware from stories in the news that many children were still at risk from monsters who, like Bill, preyed on young children. The only difference now was that there were more stories of dreadful things happening to boys as well as girls.

The first time my son went to high school, I was so afraid of him catching buses by himself. I wished I had time to take him myself, but the other boys all needed to be taken to school for nine o'clock too. His school was six miles away, so the logistics were impossible. He hadn't been at high school long when he came home telling me about the games lesson that day, and how his teacher was really nice. Instantly, the alarm bells started to ring in my mind. 'He hasn't touched you, has he?' Before I realised how bad the words sounded, they were hurtling towards my son.

'What do you mean, Mum?'

I couldn't take back the words; they had already been spoken, so I had to try to soften their meaning in some way. 'Is he friendly? You know, putting his arm round you like one of your friends would do?'

'No, Mum, don't be daft, he's my teacher. He's just great to talk to.'

'OK, love.' I watched him as he left the kitchen, trailing his school bag along the floor behind him. He was my son, my first-born, a life I have protected since he drew his first breath. I knew that if anyone tried to hurt him or any of my children I would end up in prison on a murder charge. I knew there was just no way I would allow what had happened to me to happen to any of them.

All that is left is the rest of my life, and as each day passes me by I add good memories to my memory bank. No one can steal them because they truly belong to me, created with the man I love and the family we both share.

My new memories are now outweighing the bad ones, and the old tattered box that once was full to the brim is finally crumbling away from my mind. Each day another particle of bad memory falls away, disappearing forever, never to be relived again.

Epilogue

MY FATHER BECAME very ill in 1996 when he was diagnosed with cancer in his larynx and pharynx after routine tooth removal in preparation for dentures. A couple of months later, his mouth still hadn't healed properly so he was referred to the ear, nose and throat specialist at the county hospital. After his initial consultation, he underwent twenty-eight hours of surgery after a number of growths were discovered. It was a very traumatic time. My sister, brother and I went to the hospital every visiting hour we were allowed. We were told my father would be able to drink and eat two weeks later, but things never pan out as you expect them to. Within twenty-four hours he was back in the operating theatre where he underwent a further sixteen hours of surgery. He then developed heart problems and was moved from intensive care to the coronary-care unit.

He eventually got through all the problems and he left hospital four months later without his voice but equipped with a little gadget that he put on the side of his neck. It converted the vibrations he made when he silently spoke into words we could all hear. It was a marvellous invention, but it made him sound like one of the robots you'd find in some time-travel programme on television. I hated the loss of his voice, because of all the things I remember clearly about my dad the one thing that I don't remember is what his voice sounded like. I prayed to God that, just once, I would be able to hear the voice that had been there all through my life. My prayer was never answered.

My father had a good six months, although he had spells were he was readmitted to hospital because of complications. It was on one of these stays in hospital that he was told his cancer had returned. I never really believed it had left him, but now it was in his lungs and there was nothing anyone could do. A few short months later he returned to hospital in great pain, but he never admitted that. He always put on a brave face. He came home for a couple of days and was then admitted to a hospice where he probably had the best ten days of his life since the diagnosis of cancer.

We saw him regularly every night. He was so proud to have the care and commitment of the staff there. He put his little gadget to his neck and pointed to one of the many pots of tea he had had that day. 'They treat you like royalty,' he said. 'I can have as much tea as I like, it's fantastic.' He looked so peaceful that day, the staff had managed his pain relief and for once in such a long time he looked well, if that's possible. Two days later, he slipped into a coma. I kept a vigil by his bedside, spending nights there, sitting with Carolyn and Robert watching him die, the last tiny draughts of breath drifting out of him. It was at that moment that I began recalling the events in my childhood, events that he had caused and witnessed. I talked to him silently so that the others would not hear.

'Why, Dad? Why did you do it? Why did you not stop? Why did you not help me by keeping me safe from Bill? Why didn't you talk to him, tell him what you knew, tell him to leave your daughter alone?'

I sat there listening to the pump click the next shot of morphine into him, knowing that he could die at any moment. Once my sister and brother had left the room to go and get a drink, I stood next to my father's bedside, talking to him in a gentle whisper.

'Why, Dad? I hate you for what you have done to me. You could have stopped Bill, but you didn't. You could have stopped touching me when I asked you to but you didn't. You stole my life, and cancer is paying you back.'

Within seconds, I was trying to claw the words back, trying to push them back into my breath. I sat at the side of the bed, leaned over him, kissed him gently on his forehead and apologised for what I had said. 'I'm sorry, Dad. I don't want to lose you. Please don't go.'

That morning, six days after falling into a coma, he died. My father had gone, and so had his guilt and shame.

After sitting and writing, recapturing all that has happened to me, I have to admit that at first when I actually read it out loud it all seemed so unbelievable. How could three men contribute to the destruction of a life so young? And do it without a care in the world.

I know that what happened to me is nothing new. And I know only too well it will continue to happen regardless of what I write. I just wish that one day the adults who prey on children will, just for a split second, stop and think about the effect they have on that child's life.

Children have voices; voices speak, making words that should always be listened to.

If I had succeeded when I was fourteen with my suicide attempt, I would not have discovered the people who are important to me, the people who can still love a broken, traumatised person and nurture, mend and tend their scars enough that they become whole again. My life is now full to overflowing with people who love me. I have a wonderful family, amazing sons and an astonishing husband.

I have a sister who has not only been a sister to me but a best friend. Without her, some of the years I have faced would truly have been unbearable. My family is full of people who care very deeply about me and have shown me immense love. It is through them that my strength has grown enough to face all the demons that were hiding in my box.

They have been given their eviction orders.

I hope that this book helps others who, like me, will gain their own immense strength to stand up and say: 'Stop. No more. This life belongs to me.'

Acknowledgements

MY DEEPEST GRATITUDE goes to my husband, a wonderful man who for the past twenty years has been my shoulder, my strength and my saviour. There were many nights through all of this when he gave me space alone to write. If he heard the computer keyboard being energetically tapped, he would go off and do other things, quite often at two or three in the morning. But no matter what time it was he always kept me topped up with fresh cups of tea at regular intervals!

If it weren't for your encouragement and belief in me as an individual, I don't think I would have ever become the strong person that I am today. You are truly a miracle for me: I feel blessed that you have opened up your life to become a part of mine, sharing each and every wonderful moment with me and our boys.

I love you forever.

I would also like to thank my boys. Without them, my life would have been so unfulfilled. They each have brought exceptional, precious moments that I have cherished and put in my memory box to treasure forever. You have all become such remarkable young men. Every minute of every day I truly have been blessed to be your mum. Thank you.

Thirdly, I would like to thank the other people, both family and friends, who have made memories with me that have left me aching with so much laughter inside I thought I would explode. Each one of the memories we made together added strength to my heart. Each one of you are extraordinary: my in-laws, my sister and my special friends, M-L, D, G and J, K, and S. I have been so privileged to be a part of your lives. Thank you all for all your blessings. I hope other people are as blessed by you all as I have truly been.

Finally, to Mum, remember one thing: I'll always love you.